"If you feel stuck emotional̶l̶y̶ ̶t̶h̶i̶s̶ book is for you. In *Moving* ̶F̶o̶r̶w̶a̶r̶d̶,̶ ̶J̶o̶h̶n̶ helps you identify the issues .... holding you back and equips you with specific, life-changing truth from God's Word. Unlock a new perspective, because it's time to move forward."

Craig Groeschel, pastor of Life.Church and author of *#Struggles—Following Jesus in a Selfie-Centered World*

"A life of freedom can be difficult to attain amid the chaos and distractions of everyday life. In *Moving Forward*, my friend John Siebeling shares the experiences that have freed him from these hindrances. He positions you with life-giving teachings to lay hold of God's best for your life."

John Bevere, author/minister, Messenger International

"*Moving Forward* is an eye-opening book that allows readers to realize the walls between themselves and God. John Siebeling gives outstanding points and thoughts about barriers that can hold us back in life. Siebeling also gives biblical examples of how to deal with each and every battle in life. If you are someone who wants to be closer to God but feel like you are being held back by struggles in your life, this book is perfect for you."

Matthew Barnett, cofounder of The Dream Center

"So many Christians *exist* but don't truly *live*. Instead of rooting out the junk in our lives, we often adjust to the weight of our issues, bury them deeper, and conveniently forget about them. John's incredibly valuable book *Moving Forward* does not just identify cumbersome areas that deplete our spiritual lives but also provides practical, biblical tools to help us de-clutter and change for good."

Stovall Weems, pastor of Celebration Church
and author of *The God-First Life*

"When we're young and everything we own can fit into our car, moving isn't so bad. But as we go through life we tend to accumulate more and more stuff until, eventually, the idea of moving seems overwhelming. The same thing happens in our spiritual lives; we let our baggage hold us back from living the sort of life God has for us. If that sounds like you, then check out my friend John Siebeling's new book and get ready to move!"

Greg Surratt, founding pastor of Seacoast Church

"With clarity and passion, *Moving Forward* reveals ten issues that can get you stuck in a downward spiral. If you just can't get past your past, John Siebeling won't let you down but gives clear steps for moving forward in your life."

Rick Bezet, lead pastor of New Life Church of Arkansas and author of *Be Real: Because Fake Is Exhausting*

MOVING
forward

OVERCOMING *the* HABITS, HANGUPS, *and* MISHAPS *That* HOLD YOU BACK

JOHN SIEBELING

BakerBooks

a division of Baker Publishing Group
Grand Rapids, Michigan

Published by Baker Books
a division of Baker Publishing Group
P.O. Box 6287, Grand Rapids, MI 49516-6287
www.bakerbooks.com

Printed in the United States of America

Library of Congress Cataloging-in-Publication Data is on file at the Library of Congress, Washington, DC.

ISBN 978-0-8010-1505-2

16   17   18   19   20   21   22   7   6   5   4   3   2   1

Contents

Introduction

It's Time

Yesterday is not ours to recover,
but tomorrow is ours to win or lose.

Lyndon B. Johnson

Life can be unpredictable. You don't always know what's going to come your way or what you're going to need to get through it successfully. And while this is true on a deep, philosophical level, in my early years of parenting it also took on a much more literal meaning. Especially when it came to going anywhere successfully with kids. *Especially* on road trips.

Literally, you just don't know what's going to happen in the miles between you and your destination, or what you might need to ensure a relatively smooth trip. My survival motto became "Be prepared . . . or else."

We had a Honda Odyssey van when the kids were small, and we loved it. It was awesome—it had plenty of room for everything we needed, for every foreseeable situation. There was only one problem: it had plenty of room for everything we *didn't* need too.

There was so much room it was almost like we got tricked into putting stuff in there just because we could.

I remember one particular visit to Baton Rouge that probably could have broken the record for the amount of stuff we brought per person. We brought a stroller, a high chair, an infant seat, an ExerSaucer, a Pack 'n' Play, DVDs, snack bags, coolers for baby food, diaper bags, a potted plant for Leslie's dad, and so much more—and all of our luggage, of course.

We got it all packed with no headaches from trying to decide what to cram in and what to leave at home. It was great. Granted, I couldn't see anything out of the rearview mirror because every last inch was packed with stuff, but at that point I really didn't want to stop, unpack, and have to decide what to bring and what to leave. It would be easier to just keep going.

Or so I thought.

We finally arrived at Leslie's parents' house, and thirty-eight trips later I was still bringing things into the house. Leslie's dad walked by a few times and eventually joked, "You're *still* unpacking that thing? Are y'all moving in?" It sure felt like it.

In my eagerness to get to our desired destination, I hadn't really stopped to evaluate just how much *stuff* we'd accumulated. In the process of packing for a four-day trip, we'd packed what seemed like everything we owned in the back of the van, and now I was stuck dealing with the aftermath of our let's-take-it-all packing strategy.

Junk in the Trunk

This might be somewhat of a lighthearted example, but the reality is the same thing can happen to us—not only with our cars and physical possessions but also with the "junk" we acquire in the deep places of our life. It's the unresolved hurts, the dead-weight habits, the unhealthy hangups we accumulate over the years as we go through life. It's the stuff we're not proud of . . . the things sometimes no one else can see.

Maybe resentment is constantly bubbling beneath the surface because we've been passed over for a promotion at work—again. Maybe destructive habits formed in a pressure-filled season of life are slowly stealing control of our life. Maybe the hurt of a dysfunctional relationship has marked us with constant feelings of insecurity, anger, or regret. Or perhaps there's just a lingering sense of disappointment about the way life has turned out.

So often, instead of working through these hurts and struggles as we encounter them, we push them down and try to forget about them. We put them off to deal with another day, hoping they'll resolve themselves. But instead these issues grow within us and start to seep out and impact how we handle life. As they grow, they can create all kinds of hindrances on our journey.

Imagine trying to maneuver through an obstacle course wearing a mountain-climbing backpack with a lifetime of junk spilling out of it—slowing us down, getting caught on everything we walk by, making it impossible to squeeze through some of the tight spots standing between us and the finish line.

Life has enough obstacles to navigate; we don't need to bring the junk from our past with us to add more. Whether it's

9

deep, hurtful wounds or seemingly harmless habits that have accumulated, the fact remains it's all taking up valuable space in our life. If left unaddressed these issues—the "junk in our trunk"—will steal the space intended for God's best, things like peace, hope, joy, confidence, vision, and so much more.

A lot of times these issues run deep and touch the most sensitive and vulnerable parts of our heart. The messy, cluttered, tangled up parts that are uncomfortable to admit, and even more uncomfortable to deal with. So we tell ourselves our junked-up heart isn't really a big deal.

But actually it is.

Why? *Because God has something better for us.*

An Uncluttered Heart

Some people go their entire lives dissatisfied with life as they know it but unaware it could be any different. I want to encourage you, friend: *it can.* As we go through life, we will inevitably encounter challenges, temptations, and obstacles. The good news is we don't have to let them be the defining forces in our life. As Romans 8:37 reminds us, "Despite all this, overwhelming victory is ours through Christ who loved us enough to die for us" (TLB).

God has called us to live an overcoming life—to rise above anything weighing us down or holding us back from experiencing his best. He doesn't want our "junk" to bring us to a standstill. He doesn't want it to define us and dominate us. He wants us to have freedom and forward motion in our life. That's what this book is all about.

In 1 Chronicles, David prays a powerful prayer for his son Solomon. The greatest endeavor of Solomon's life was before him as he prepared to build the temple that would house the presence of God. David fully understood the role Solomon's heart could play in determining whether the outcome was a success or failure.

"And give my son Solomon *an uncluttered and focused heart*," David prayed, "so that he can obey what you command, live by your directions and counsel, and carry through with building The Temple for which I have provided" (1 Chron. 29:19 MSG, emphasis added).

It's hard to live an overcoming life with a cluttered, distracted heart. If we truly want to embrace the fullness of what God has called us to, it's going to mean digging deep into our heart and mind and clearing out the clutter.

We see three things that come from an uncluttered heart:

1. **The ability to obey God's commands.** (Receiving the strength and willpower to choose what's right and reject what's wrong.)
2. **The ability to live by God's directions and counsel.** (Hearing God's voice and taking godly principles and wisdom to heart so we make wise choices in living and managing our everyday lives.)
3. **The ability to carry out the purposes attached to our life.** (Drawing out the potential God has placed within us and accomplishing what he created us for.)

So many of us have good intentions and want to fulfill our calling in life, but we get distracted, give up when things get tough, or get hijacked by personal issues and challenges that weren't dealt with along the way.

If we want to accomplish all God has called us to *do*, we have to first focus on becoming who he's called us to *be*. An uncluttered heart gives us the internal strength to keep moving forward and keep making progress over the long haul.

An Inside Job

No one—and I mean *no one*—is immune to having junk in his or her trunk. Not you. Not me. Not anyone. We all have issues. If you think you don't have issues . . . that's probably your issue!

Sometimes the people who appear to have it the most together are the most hurting and broken inside. It's ok to admit you don't have it all together, because none of us do.

God can bring freedom and order to even the messiest, most impossible-looking places in our life. It doesn't matter if it's something simple like becoming a better manager of our time or something complicated like breaking free from an addiction that has been running our life for decades. No matter what the issue is, we can overcome it with God's help. But true freedom is about more than just modifying external behavior; it's about fixing the issue from the inside out.

In his honest and insightful book *Ordering Your Private World*, Gordon MacDonald talks about the incredibly important role our inner life plays in positioning us to be free and fulfill our potential. As a young man, Gordon was one of those standout individuals everyone knew was destined for success. And as the years went on, by all measurable, visible standards he was achieving that success as a young pastor, husband, and father.

But underneath it all, his inner world was chaotic and disordered. Eventually the weight of his responsibilities pushed him to his breaking point. In a raw, painful moment one Saturday morning, he came to the sobering realization that he'd neglected his inner world for too long. It was clear that unless he addressed the chaos and disorder of his internal life, he would never achieve his full potential, and most likely his world would eventually self-destruct.

In the preface of his book he shares a poignant truth he learned in that painful but life-changing season:

> The order of my private world is an inside-out matter, not an outside-in matter. We are all so tempted to buy gadgets . . . with the hopes that they will bring tidiness of life. But it doesn't work that way. Forget the gadgets and start with the interior, private world. The order we seek begins with a thorough scouring of the inside of life. With tough questions that it may take others to help us answer. With a confronting of beliefs and principles that are toxic and destructive. With a listening to the voice of God who has better for us.[1]

God's solution for change starts with a willingness to admit the messes in our life and bring them into direct contact with him—his presence, his power, his Word. He heals wounded hearts, puts broken spirits back together, and restores hope to the discouraged and disillusioned. He lifts burdens and supplies strength for the weary. Our God is a God who specializes in transformation and restoration.

The level of health and order we have inside of us determines how we handle the situations, opportunities, challenges, and relationships we have in the present. That, in turn, determines the level of long-term health and success we have in our future.

What's inside matters. For me. For you. For those around us. For our future and all God has called us to be.

Moving Forward

The limiting factors in our present do not have to be the determining factors for our future. Because of Christ's death on the cross, there is a new, different future waiting for us to step into it.

The Message paraphrase of Romans 8:1–2 paints a powerful picture of the freedom God has made available to us through Jesus:

> With the arrival of Jesus, the Messiah, that fateful dilemma is resolved. Those who enter into Christ's being-here-for-us no longer have to live under a continuous, low-lying black cloud. A new power is in operation. The Spirit of life in Christ, like a strong wind, has magnificently cleared the air, freeing you from a fated lifetime of brutal tyranny at the hands of sin and death.

When we live under the weight of persistent issues and struggles, it really does feel like we are living "under a continuous, low-lying black cloud." The shadow cast over our life can start to become part of our identity—who we are and how we do life. But Jesus came to clear the air and set us free. We no longer have to settle for a life run by our sins and weaknesses.

· · · · · ·

I wrote this book because I've seen too many people living beneath the weight of problems and hangups that God has a solution for in his Word. But I've also seen how dramatically a life can change when God's truth is consistently put into action.

This book is for anyone who's ready to move forward in life, whether you're already making good progress or are completely stuck. In it, we'll look together at some of the most common issues that can take up valuable space in your life and prevent you from receiving God's best. We'll unpack God's Word to find his solutions for overcoming them and walking in true freedom.

Every one may not be a hot-button issue for you, but I hope you'll read each chapter with an engaged heart. Principles from God's Word can often help us find wisdom for dealing with other areas of our life or open our understanding to what others are walking through.

As you read, take your time. Pause. Listen for the still, small voice of the Holy Spirit. Ask God to help you recognize any area of your life that might need some decluttering. Author and organizational expert Kathi Lipp makes a profound statement about the physical, tangible areas of our life, but it applies to the spiritual area of our life as well: "At its heart, clutter is a lack of peace."[2]

God's principles bring order and peace into the cluttered, chaotic places of our life as we implement them. Let me encourage you to purpose in your heart to follow through on whatever the Holy Spirit leads you to do.

This book will provide practical, manageable steps to help you overcome the issues holding you back. But more importantly, I pray it will paint a picture of the freedom and purpose that are possible through Jesus and ignite a desire to pursue them—and him—relentlessly.

So if you're ready to embrace the possibilities, to write a new chapter in your story, and to begin moving forward, let's get started.

It's time.

Before we move on, I encourage you to take a moment to talk honestly with God about any area of your life that may be holding you back. You can use your own words or pray this simple prayer:

Dear God, I want to overcome anything holding me back from being who you've called me to be and doing all you've called me to do. Speak to me about the things I need to change. Help me open my heart and life unreservedly to you—even the deepest, most vulnerable areas I've kept closed off. I give you permission to do exactly what you need to do. Give me the courage to start doing what I need to do and the strength to walk it out to completion. Amen.

one

The Blame Game

The price of greatness is responsibility.

Winston Churchill

Actor Steve Carell once said, "Goalies almost never get credit for winning a game, but they always get blamed for losing a game."[1] I can tell you from personal experience: this is 100 percent true.

I played soccer in ninth and tenth grade, and we were a great team—in fact, we were state champs. I remember one particular game against one of the best teams in the state. It was 0–0 going into the last few minutes of the game, and one of our opponents kicked the ball. It hit my teammate's leg and made a slapping noise. The referee called "hand ball," which meant a penalty kick in the last minute of the game. If you know anything about soccer and penalty kicks, it's the hardest thing to defend. It's just one-on-one with the goalkeeper, who happened to be me. You can imagine the rest of the story. I dove one way and the ball went the other way. 1–0, they won.

The game ended and we all walked off the field. I was so mad at the ref. His mistake robbed us of the win we deserved. The more I thought about it, the angrier I got.

I climbed in the car with my dad and started complaining about the referee and the call he'd made. You know what my dad's response was? He said, "How many opportunities did you guys have to win the game? Plenty. You can't blame the ref." He proceeded to give me a twenty-minute speech about blaming refs, blaming other people, and losing well.

I was furious. My dad was a smart man, and being a college professor, he loved to pass on his wisdom to us in the form of lectures. The whole time he was talking, I acted like I wasn't listening, but the truth is, I heard every word. (*Parents, take note—your kids are listening more than you might think!*) To this day, when a player loses a game and blames the ref in a press conference, it drives me crazy. I know there are bad calls sometimes, but part of me wants to say, "Stop blaming someone else. Man up!"

There are always going to be times when things don't go our way, something unfair happens, or we find ourselves in the middle of circumstances we can't control. While we might not be responsible for creating them, we are responsible for how we react to them.

I love how pastor Charles Swindoll talks about this in a simple essay called "Attitudes."

Words can never adequately convey the incredible impact of our attitude toward life. The longer I live the more convinced I become that life is 10 percent what happens to us and 90 percent how we respond to it.

I believe the single most significant decision I can make on a day-to-day basis is my choice of attitude. It is more important than my past, my education, my bankroll, my successes or failures, fame or pain, what other people think of me or say about me, my circumstances, or my position. Attitude keeps me going or cripples my progress. It alone fuels my fire or assaults my hope. When my attitudes are right, there's no barrier too high, no valley too deep, no dream too extreme, no challenge too great for me.[2]

We may think the people who get the lucky breaks and ideal circumstances handed to them are the ones with the advantage in life. But the truth is, your attitude is what gives you the advantage. No matter the circumstances, the person with a positive, can-do spirit has the advantage every time.

The Devil Made Me Do It

Blame is one of the most destructive emotions that keeps people from living a full and free life. In fact, what makes blame even more powerful is that if we allow it to sneak into our perspective, even just a little, it will grow into a full-blown mentality that impacts every part of our life.

In Genesis 3, we see the story of how Adam and Eve gave in to temptation and ate the fruit God told them not to. Sin entered God's perfect, flawless creation for the first time. It was the moment that changed everything.

After they ate it, Adam and Eve immediately knew they had done something wrong. As we read the story, it seems Adam and Eve would walk with God each evening. But this night was different. God went to meet them but they weren't there. They were hiding in the bushes, filled with shame. God calls out to them, and an interesting dialog between God, Adam, and Eve begins:

> But the LORD God called to the man, "Where are you?"
>
> He answered, "I heard you in the garden, and I was afraid because I was naked; so I hid."
>
> And he said, "Who told you that you were naked? Have you eaten from the tree that I commanded you not to eat from?"
>
> The man said, "The woman you put here with me—she gave me some fruit from the tree, and I ate it."
>
> Then the LORD God said to the woman, "What is this you have done?"
>
> The woman said, "The serpent deceived me, and I ate." (vv. 9–13)

Adam and Eve's first reaction when they were caught was to look for someone to blame. Sin steps into the world—and right on its heels is blame. I think it's important to notice the connection. Where one is, the other is not far behind.

God asks if they've eaten from the tree he told them not to—it's a simple yes or no question. Instead of answering, Adam starts grasping for a "reason." "Uh, well, you see, God . . . that woman . . . you know, God, the woman *you* put here with me? Well, she gave me some fruit from the tree, and I ate it." Then God turns to Eve to hear her side of the story, and she points the finger at the snake and says, "He tricked me into eating it!" They immediately looked to displace responsibility for their actions.

The Buck Stops Here

For many people, a blame-based perspective is the single greatest factor keeping them stuck in life. A desire to displace responsibility will always sabotage our success in life. You may have heard the saying, "Excuses are the nails used to build a house of failure." If we're serious about moving forward, we need to do some renovation work on the foundation of our life—the core beliefs and mentalities that drive us. We've got to break down and remove any blame-based mindsets so that we can have a solid foundation to build on.

Blame Buster 1:
I am responsible for my life.

Sometimes we need to stop and say this to ourselves: *I am responsible for my life.* That means I'm responsible for my attitude. I'm responsible for my finances. I'm responsible for my choices. *I'm responsible.* This is a foundational principle we have to embrace if we're going to live the life God wants us to live.

Think honestly about your life and how often you may be preventing success in a certain area because you are making excuses for the state things are in. Is there any area of your life you wish was further along or in a better position? It could be your mood. It could be your marriage. It could be your career. Ask yourself, *Is there an excuse I am standing behind? Am I blaming someone or something for the condition of that particular area of my life?*

The truth is, our excuses will excuse success from our life. Author and productivity consultant Denis Waitley puts it this way: "There are two primary choices in life: accept conditions as they exist or accept the responsibility for changing them."[3] Responsibility allows us to close the gap between where we are and where we want to be.

Blame Buster 2:
Blame is the hallmark of unfulfilled potential.

When we make an excuse or place blame, we're displacing responsibility. We're taking responsibility away from ourselves and placing it in the hands of someone or something else. The biggest problem is that as we hand them the responsibility, we are also handing them the power over our life. When we blame, we actually empower the person or thing we are blaming.

I think it's so interesting that the original Greek word in the New Testament for *sin* means "to miss the mark," and the original word for *excuse* means "a reason to miss the mark."

The mark is God's plan and his purpose for our life. It's being the person God has called us to be and living the thriving, overcoming life God has called us to live.

A lot of times we're tempted to turn a blind eye to the issues in our life that hold us back. But the truth is, that's not really a luxury we have. James 4:17 says if we know the good we ought to do, and don't do it, that's sin. We need to deal swiftly with anything that's hindering us. Choosing to settle for less than God's best causes us to miss the mark. When we blame and make excuses, we find ourselves trapped in a vicious cycle.

If we stay on that track, ultimately we will develop a victim mentality, which will always keep us focused on the problem and on ourselves. When this happens, we can't see the better future God planned for us.

In his book *No Excuses!*, Brian Tracy says:

> As long as you are blaming someone else for something in your life you don't like, you will remain a "mental child."

You continue to see yourself as small and helpless, like a victim. You continue to lash out. However, when you begin to accept responsibility . . . you transform yourself into a "mental adult." You will see yourself as being in charge of your own life, and no longer a victim.[4]

For many of us, this requires a major shift in our thinking. Blame elevates people and situations above the power of God placed inside you. When we think of it that way, then we can recognize this type of thinking is totally contrary to what the Word of God says. First John 4:4 reminds us that "the Spirit in you is far greater than anything in the world" (MSG).

Instead of seeing ourselves as a victim of our circumstances, we need to see ourselves with the potential God sees in us— to be strong, capable, and able to make good decisions. The moment we take responsibility is the moment we have started on the path to success.

Blame Buster 3:
Blame will rob me. Accepting responsibility will arm me.

Blame always takes, but accepting responsibility always gives. Accepting responsibility may not be the easy route, and it may not feel good in the moment, but it will always be the option that moves our life forward the most in the long run.

In Luke 14, Jesus tells a simple story we can learn a lot from. It's about a man who was preparing a great feast. He invited many people, but when the servant went to confirm their RSVPs, they started to back out one by one.

> But they all alike began to make excuses. The first said, "I have just bought a field, and I must go and see it. Please excuse me."

Another said, "I have just bought five yoke of oxen, and I'm on my way to try them out. Please excuse me."

Still another said, "I just got married, so I can't come."

The servant came back and reported this to his master. Then the owner of the house became angry and ordered his servant, "Go out quickly into the streets and alleys of the town and bring in the poor, the crippled, the blind and the lame."

"Sir," the servant said, "what you ordered has been done, but there is still room."

Then the master told his servant, "Go out to the roads and country lanes and compel them to come in, so that my house will be full. I tell you, not one of those who were invited will get a taste of my banquet." (vv. 18–24)

Jesus is giving us an illustration about the kingdom of God and the great things God has for you and me. The master prepared all kinds of wonderful things for his guests, but they excused themselves from the opportunity to receive them. We see three attitudes that produced excuses and robbed them of the blessing available to them: pride, disrespect, and complacency. Responsibility, in contrast, arms us with humility, respect, and determination.

Responsibility arms us with humility.

One of the first things we can notice in this passage is how self-focused all of these people are. More than any other word, we see the word *I.* "I have . . . I must . . . I have . . . I'm on my way . . . I just . . . I can't."

When we're focused on ourselves there is a sense of pride, and pride paves the way for destruction in our life (Prov. 16:18). It keeps us from seeing any faults in ourselves—it's always someone else's fault. *It's my father's fault, the way he raised us . . . It's the school system's fault . . . It's my wife's fault . . . It's my personality . . . It's my kids . . . It's my boss . . .* If we stop and think about it, though, isn't it pretty prideful to think we have nothing to do with any of the challenges we're facing?

Jim Collins, author of *Good to Great* and renowned business management researcher, talks about "level five" leaders—the highest caliber executives who have been found to possess two distinct, defining characteristics: extreme personal humility and intense professional will. The other characteristics common to this elite group of leaders were a ferocious resolve and the tendency to give credit to others while assigning blame to themselves.[5]

Pride creates resistance and roadblocks to success in our life, but a willingness to take responsibility does just the opposite. As 1 Peter 5:5 tells us, "God opposes the proud but shows favor to the humble." A humble spirit will create momentum and give us the God-advantage in life.

Responsibility arms us with respect.

When we read this story, it seems these guys had been invited previously and had accepted the invitation. The servant was sent out to gather those who had been invited and had accepted. But now, even though they had said yes before, they were backing out. Their disrespect for the host who'd invited them undoubtedly cost them his respect.

By choosing to accept responsibility in the small, practical, and everyday areas of our life, we will begin to earn the respect of others and gain a sense of self-respect. What exactly does that look like? Here are some very simple but very important ways we need to take responsibility in our everyday lives.

- **Be able to admit we're wrong—and apologize.** People are so much quicker to give respect to someone who will admit they messed up, take responsibility for their actions, offer an apology, and then start working to make things right. (And just for the record, "Oops, my bad!" doesn't count as an apology!) Humble yourself enough to look someone in the eye and genuinely say, "I made a mistake. I'm sorry. Will you please forgive me?"

- **Follow through with our commitments.** This is one of the most significant things we can do to build a life of respect. Not only respect from other people but also self-respect. If you say you're going to be there, be there. If you say you are going to do it, do it. Be someone who is faithful, who honors their word, and who can be counted on.

- **Take care of our business.** Life requires regular maintenance. It's our job to be responsible for taking care of it. If you get a bill and it's due in thirty days, do everything in your power to pay it on time, even if it is the twenty-ninth day. Take good care of your home, your car, and the things you've been blessed with. When you've spent all your eating out money, brown bag it at work.

Taking responsibility—in both the little things and the big things—is essential if we want to build a healthy, successful life. It isn't always fun or exciting, but faithfulness positions us to reap significant benefits and rewards across the different areas of our life.

Responsibility arms us with determination.

When we're living in a place of blame and always making excuses, it kills our appetite to move forward. It removes the drive to make something of our life, because if it's always someone else's fault, there is never anything we can do to improve our situation. We will always be waiting for someone else to fix our life for us.

It's ok to "not be ok" or need help in different seasons in life. God designed us to need people and not to go through life alone. But we can't ever put the responsibility for our happiness, joy, or health on someone else. You might have heard it said this way: "Don't put the key to your happiness in someone else's pocket." It's not fair to you, and it's not fair to them.

I know some of us have been left to pick up the pieces or bear the scars of someone else's devastating choices. You are living with daily reminders of the consequences of their actions. Maybe you'd even go so far as to say, "They ruined my life." My heart is not to minimize the pain you may have experienced at the hands of others. But don't let those hurts and wrongdoings cause further damage to your future by allowing them to produce a victim mentality in your spirit.

For your own sake, and for the sake of your future, I want to encourage you with this: no matter how hard it may seem, don't let *victim* become a part of your identity. *Victor* and *victim* both have the same Latin prefix, *vic*, which means to "win, conquer."[6] The difference in the words is in who does the conquering. We can let our circumstances conquer us, or we can choose to rise up and remember that "in all these things *we are more than conquerors* through him who loved us" (Rom. 8:37, emphasis added).

Maya Angelou shares a collection of the most valuable lessons learned in her lifetime in her book *Letter to My Daughter*. Among them is this wise reminder: "You may not control all the events that happen to you, but you can decide not to be reduced by them."[7] A victim mentality steals our edge. We lose our desire to rise up and make a difference, to hit the mark and be all God wants us to be. But when we accept responsibility for our life, there is a sense of hunger and motivation to rise up, because we realize we have the opportunity to change our life!

In his book *The 7 Habits of Highly Effective People*, leadership expert Stephen Covey says, "Our behavior is a product of our decisions, not our conditions."[8] I wholeheartedly agree. Our circumstances do not have the power to control our life unless we allow them to. We can decide what the next chapter of our story will be! The reality is, we've been given the *chance* to change, but we have to make the *choice* to change. It won't just happen.

Life has a way of sucking the wind out of our sails. Wearing down our resolve. Lulling us into a place where it's easier to just stop caring. We feel too tired from the frenzied pace of daily life, too discouraged from the setbacks, and too overwhelmed by the issues and problems that have worked themselves into our life. If we're not careful, complacency can creep into our heart.

Complacency and blame usually go hand in hand. When we're complacent, the goal and the vision slip out of focus. We start letting our responsibilities slide. We start drifting off track. And when that happens, it's easy to start blaming something or someone else for the negative results. When that happens, we're on the edge of a slippery slope.

Complacency will always choose convenience over commitment. It may feel comfortable today, but it could eventually cost you your future.

· · · · · ·

Remember those guests in the story Jesus told? We are in a similar situation. God has extended an invitation to you and me. It's an invitation to a life bigger than ourselves, attached to a divine purpose and shaped for a significant calling. The decision is up to us: *Are we backing out or are we pressing in?*

So many times, blame is a fallback rooted in fear. We're afraid to face the truth, to admit our own shortcomings. Afraid of the pain change may bring or the risk of stepping out into the unknown. It's easier to sit back and blame someone or something else for our problems instead of going through the discomfort of trying to solve them. So in some ways, yes, blame feels safe, but really it isn't safe at all. We're choosing comfort at the expense of our destiny.

Blame is always a barrier to God's best. Don't let excuses rob you of your future. Make the decision to embrace responsibility. Let it arm you with what you need to take hold of God's best for your life. The weight of responsibility strengthens us today so we can carry the load of our destiny tomorrow.

Evaluate / Eliminate / Elevate

Evaluate: Are there areas of your life you have been viewing with a blame-based perspective?

Eliminate: While some situations may not be within your control, consider the aspects of your life that are within your power to change. Are there excuses you have been standing behind?

Elevate: What changes do you need to make? Use the statement below to create specific steps toward action.

- *I am responsible for*

  _____

  (my health, attitude, habits, and so forth).

- *I won't stand behind the excuse of*

  _____ *anymore.*

- *I choose to take responsibility by*

  _____

  (action step).

two

Steady On

A victorious person does not have
the luxury of living by feelings.

Joyce Meyer

I think one of the places God does the most character building
for me is in the car. There's nothing like hitting every red light
for five miles when you're late for a meeting (or slow drivers
who insist on being in the fast lane) to test your self-control!

I remember one particular incident when I was driving to
the mall with my daughter, who was probably around four
years old. Somehow I managed to make the guy driving next
to me really, really angry. He pulled closer and screamed at
me from his car, obviously enraged. In an instant, indigna-
tion, frustration, and anger all rose up inside me.

I wish I could say I just pulled my car over and had a little
moment of prayer for him, or at least ignored him. But I didn't.

I yelled right back. I was *so* mad. How on earth could he be getting that worked up? And as we kept driving he just stayed right with me and we just kept on yelling at each other.

From the backseat, in the midst of it all, I heard my daughter's little voice asking, "What's going on? Why is that man mad, Daddy? Why is he yelling at you?" It wasn't my proudest moment, to say the least!

The next morning I stopped at Starbucks on my way into the office. I looked up and I couldn't believe it. The same man was standing right there in Starbucks. We kind of looked at each other with that look that says, *Do I know you from somewhere?*

I don't think he realized where he recognized me from, but I knew exactly who he was. I got my latte as quickly as I could and got out of there. As heated as our exchange was the day before, I wasn't too eager to stick around and see if he'd connect the dots. As I was hurrying to my car, I couldn't help but wonder how things might have gone down if he'd remembered where he recognized me from!

· · · · · ·

The British have a great phrase, "Steady on," that's often interjected to someone who is getting caught up in their emotions. It's a nautical reference, derived from a captain's instructions to the helmsman to "hold your course" or "steer steady" in the face of some kind of disrupting event.

It eventually evolved and made its way into everyday language as an expression to tell people not to get carried away with their emotions and act foolishly. Across the pond in England they might say it means, "Don't act precipitously." American translation: "Check yourself before you wreck yourself."

It's so easy to let ourselves get carried away by our emotions sometimes, even over things that aren't a big deal, just like my little driving incident. Logically, I knew some guy getting mad in traffic wasn't that big of a deal, but somehow that didn't stop my emotions from taking over in the moment. When emotions get the best of us, they bring out the worst in us.

It's no wonder this nautical term, "steady on," started to be used in reference to our feelings. They can bear quite a resemblance to the sea—capable of being calm and serene, unpredictable and tempestuous, and everything in between.

However, the waters, whether calm or violent, are not intended to be the determining force in the ship's journey. A ship left to the force of the water around it will drift off course or be overtaken by the storms. It will never reach its intended destination.

In the same way, God didn't design our feelings to chart the course of our journey through life. No matter what emotions are pressing around us on our journey, the best course of action is *steady on*. Hold our course, don't waver, and keep steering steady as we move forward.

* * * * *

When our emotions are calling the shots, their uneven rhythm seems to creep into every part of our life. They can disrupt our stability and cause us to be all over the map, because emotions tell us to do what feels good, not necessarily what will move us forward in life.

Proverbs 25:28 warns us about the danger of letting our feelings lead: "Like a city that is broken down and without walls [leaving it unprotected] is a man who has no self-control over his spirit [and sets himself up for trouble]" (AMP). Any area of our life controlled by our feelings is vulnerable to getting off track.

When our feelings are in charge, we quit when the job gets tough. We check out when the relationship gets a little rocky. We get discouraged easily or avoid taking risks because we're afraid to fail. We procrastinate because we don't "feel" like doing it. We are quick to get frustrated and display it with sharp words and angry sighs.

The reality is, our feelings will drive decisions in every area of our life if we let them—even areas we may not realize are being impacted by our feelings. We *feel like* eating an entire bag of Doritos . . . so we do. We *don't feel like* getting up earlier so we can be on time . . . so we don't. When we really think about it, many of the hangups, frustrations, and challenges holding us back in life boil down to letting our feelings and emotions be in control of our decisions.

What exactly are these intangible yet unexplainably powerful forces called *emotions*? How can they influence us so strongly and even seem to initiate a hostile takeover, incapacitating our common sense at times? And moreover, how do we handle our emotions so they're not handling us?

To get to the answer, we have to dig down below the surface and take a look at what's happening underneath. I'm not necessarily a mechanically inclined person, but I have found that if we want to fix something it helps to have a basic understanding of how it functions.

A Crazy Little Thing Called Feelings

Our feelings are the emotions attached to our thoughts.[1] We have conscious thoughts we recognize, acknowledge, and put words to, even if those words are only in our mind. But we also have subconscious thoughts—thoughts we have not fully formulated or processed in the context of words. This is why, when you hear something hurtful, you can respond emotionally before you're able to find any words—anger can rise up or tears can fall immediately. The thought is there, even if the words are not.

If we are feeling a lot of negative emotions, it means we are having a lot of negative thoughts, either consciously or subconsciously. Emotions help give us information about what we are truly thinking. The problem is, what we think isn't always true. As Neil T. Anderson says in his book *Victory Over the Darkness*, "If what you think does not reflect the truth, then what you feel does not reflect reality."[2]

For example, if we believe our worth is based on our appearance or achievements, we begin to feel less valuable when we fail to meet that flawed standard. But the truth is, no matter what we *feel* to be true, our value never increases or decreases based on our achievements or appearance. Our true value is based on one thing: our identity as a son or daughter of God. It's crucial that we continually seek out God's truth through his Word, the Bible, and align our thoughts with it. Otherwise we can begin to build thoughts based on inaccurate information.

Our thoughts and emotions are very closely intertwined, and they influence each other and our body significantly. God's Word has been telling us for thousands of years the depth of the connection between our mind, our body, and our emotions. "A sound mind makes for a robust body, but runaway emotions corrode the bones" (Prov. 14:30 MSG).

Science is increasingly coming to the same conclusion! Dr. Candace Pert made significant contributions to neuroscience in her lifetime through her pioneering work in stress research and the connection between the mind, emotions, and the body. She said, "In the beginning of my work, I matter-of-factly presumed that emotions were in the head or the brain. Now I would say they are really in the body."[3]

What this means is our emotions are not just intangible sensations we experience in our "heart" and "mind." In fact, quite the opposite: we experience our emotions in the form of chemical reactions in our brain and in our body—from our organs, such as the heart, stomach, and so on, down to our individual cells.[4]

The more the scientific community studies the connection between the mind and the body, the more it confirms God's Word: what we feel emotionally impacts how we feel physically. Researchers have scientifically linked emotions to high blood pressure, diseases of the immune system, and cardiovascular disease. Studies show infections, allergies, and autoimmune diseases are also highly influenced by emotions. Also, emotions such as depression are linked to an increased risk for cancer and heart disease.

One study conducted over ten years showed people who were not able to manage their emotional stress had a 40 percent higher death rate than people who were not stressed. Harvard Medical School studied over 1,500 heart attack survivors and found individuals who experienced anger brought on by emotional conflicts had double the risk of subsequent heart attacks as opposed to individuals who stayed calm.[5]

The far-reaching effects of our emotions (especially negative ones) are much greater than most of us realize. But God created us, and he knew what a powerful impact they could have on our life. This is why the Bible is filled with insight and wisdom that tells us how to manage our heart, our mind, and our emotions in a healthy way.

The Transfer That Changes Everything

Sometimes the emotional area of our life can feel very complex—perhaps even confusing or overwhelming at times. First Thessalonians 5 has some important verses that can help us understand how we've been created and how we're wired as people. Verse 23 says, "May God himself, the God of peace, sanctify you through and through. May your whole spirit, soul and body be kept blameless at the coming of our Lord Jesus Christ."

In this verse we see that God created us as a three-part being. Each part plays a unique and essential role in our life. Our spirit is the part of us that lives forever. It's the part that is saved and instantly made new when we become a Christian. Our soul is made up of our mind, our emotions, and our will. Our body obviously is our physical being that houses the spirit and the soul. Since we are a three-part being, it's important we take a whole-person approach—spirit, soul, and body—as we work on areas of our life that need freedom.

When we become a Christian, a spiritual transaction takes place. God has "rescued us from the kingdom of darkness and transferred us into the Kingdom of his dear Son, who purchased our freedom and forgave our sins" (Col. 1:13–14 NLT). Our spirit is set free from the consequences of our sin—separation from God. We don't have to live in bondage to sin or the other unhealthy things that used to dominate our life. Our freedom has been paid for, and spiritually we have been transferred out of our old way of life!

When I was fifteen, I got my very first job at a new res-taurant opening in Baton Rouge called Fuddruckers. I was a busboy, so when people were finished with their meals I'd clear the tables and get them ready for the next customer. I had a really laid-back manager named Brian, and we all just kind of stood around and hung out when there weren't any tables to bus. It was a chilled-out, low-stress job. I guess I did pretty well, because after a while they transferred me—to the bakery, of all places. The bakery department was a whole different world.

Instead of picking up after customers, I was now respon-sible for preparing the food they ate. Instead of wiping down tables, I was mixing up batches of bread and cookies. To be honest, it was all pretty foreign to me as a fifteen-year-old boy. I had no experience cooking or baking. I'd gotten fairly familiar with how to be a busboy, but that didn't help me out much after I was transferred. I was under different leadership, with a new role and new assignment. I had to learn a whole new way of doing things in order to thrive.

Culture Shock

The same thing happens to us when we become a Christian. Just as my transfer put me in a new department with a new manager, we, too, are under different leadership. When we come into the new kingdom, there's a paradigm shift that needs to take place as well. We have a new standard of right and wrong, a new source of power, a new motivation, and new goals. Our feelings are no longer in charge.

This is one of the most significant mindsets we have to shift in order to thrive in our Christian journey. Sometimes we try to carry our old way of doing things into our new life, because even though our spirit is renewed instantly, our soul is not. We still have the same mind, the same emotions, and the same will as we did before we got saved. That's where the disconnect comes for a lot of people. We can't move forward and build momentum in our new life with our old ways. Since we've been transferred, we need to develop a whole new way of approaching life.

When my wife, Leslie, and I were a young married couple, we served as missionaries in Nairobi, Kenya, for three years. I remember how much adjustment it required. So many things felt awkward and unnatural. Driving was especially hard to get used to. According to everything I'd experienced in life up to that point, everyone in Kenya was driving on the "wrong" side of the road. The steering wheel was on the "wrong" side of the car. I can't tell you how many times I went to get in the car to drive only to realize I was at the passenger door!

Kenya was a different kingdom with a different source of authority, and with it came completely new ways of doing things. As much as I felt like I wanted to drive on the other side of the road because it was familiar, it was easier, and it felt safer, it actually would have been a big mistake. Think of all the consequences: I could have wrecked the car, gotten injured, and created all kinds of problems for myself (and others), costing me time, money, and frustration—not to mention I would be prevented from getting wherever I was trying to go!

Sometimes, even though we've been transferred into God's kingdom, we keep going back to our old ways of doing things—back to when our feelings were in charge and we did whatever we wanted. But our old ways just don't work in the new kingdom. They leave us feeling unsatisfied, frustrated, and stuck. Instead, we have to look to something different to guide our choices: God's Word.

Refurbishing the Soul

Even though our spirit is instantly renewed and set free when we become a Christian, our soul is a whole different story. It needs work. *A whole lot of work.* Just because we became a Christian, it doesn't mean our thought patterns instantly change, our emotional baggage just goes away, or our bad habits magically disappear.

This is where the process of sanctifying our soul comes in. Remember what Paul said in 1 Thessalonians 5:23: "May God himself, the God of peace, sanctify you through and through. May your whole spirit, soul and body be kept blameless at the coming of our Lord Jesus Christ." When the Bible talks about sanctification, it's referring to the process of becoming more like Jesus. The word *sanctify* also means "to restore back to its original condition for its original purpose."[6] Like refurbishing a broken machine to restore it back to proper working order, sanctification is a "refurbishing" process for our soul.

God takes the components of our soul—our thinking, our feeling, and our choosing—and begins restoring them so they function as they were intended to. Notice the Scripture says "through and through." This speaks to the fact that sanctification is a process—it doesn't happen overnight and God won't do it all on his own. It's layer by layer, little by little, as we open our life to the work of the Holy Spirit and choose to align our life with the instructions found in God's Word.

Finding Freedom

There is so much to say on the subject of how to have healthy, Spirit-led emotions, but let's focus on three foundational statements to help us better understand the role emotions play in our life and set ourselves up to succeed on our journey of overcoming our "junk" and moving forward.

> *Statement 1: Consistent freedom and victory are not possible unless we learn to live beyond our feelings.*

The truth is, some people spend their lives never living beyond what they feel. God gave us emotions to help us experience life, but he never intended for them to be in charge. We may not be locked in to some deep, dark sin, but if we're a slave to our feelings, we aren't truly free. As Dallas Willard says in his book *Renovation of the Heart*, "Feelings are, with a few exceptions, good servants. But they are disastrous masters."[7]

I would venture to say that 50 percent, maybe even 75 percent, of the problems most people are dealing with are the result of letting their feelings be in charge. Feelings are most people's biggest obstacle to fulfilling their potential. A lot of people have the *potential* to be successful—the ideas, the skills, the opportunities. Usually those who actually *become* successful are those who choose to rise above their feelings and consistently do what needs to be done *in spite of how they feel*. This applies in pretty much every area of our life—spiritually, relationally, professionally, physically, and the list goes on.

Many people never move forward in life because they can't make decisions outside of how they feel. They only do what they feel like doing. Feelings will never produce an accurate road map to God's destiny for our life. We can't rely on them for our source of direction. The best God has created *in* us—and *for* us—will be discovered and drawn out as we consistently choose to live according to God's Word, not our feelings.

A Conflict of Interest

How do we stop the cycle of letting our emotions be in charge of our decisions? A great place to start is to focus on our responses. We may not be able to control which emotions we experience, but we *can* control how we respond to them. In fact, we *must*. It's our responsibility and no one else's. In the heat of raw emotion, step back and remind yourself, *I am responsible for my response.*

Responding to our emotions in a healthy, God-honoring way is the starting point for creating change. How we respond to our emotions—whether negative or positive—triggers a chain reaction. It determines the direction of our thoughts. Our thoughts influence our choices, and our choices shape our future.

When we choose a healthy response to our emotions, we're setting ourselves up for good things in our future. But let's be honest: even if we want to do what's right, it's so difficult sometimes. As Jesus said in Matthew 26:41, "The spirit is willing, but the flesh is weak." This is a struggle we are all familiar with.

We have the spirit, which we just talked about, but we also have "the flesh"—the old sinful nature. When we become a Christian, the Holy Spirit comes to live inside us, but the old sinful nature we were born with doesn't go away or instantly change. As a result, the spirit and the flesh are in constant conflict with each other.

Sometimes getting control of our flesh (especially our feelings) can feel like a losing battle. Paul wrote in Romans 7:15, "I do not understand myself. I want to do what is right but I do not do it. Instead, I do the very thing I hate" (NLV). Can you relate? I know I can.

How can we undo the hostile takeover of the flesh and start making good decisions, even when we don't feel like it? Paul gives us the answer:

> Do not be deceived: God cannot be mocked. A man reaps what he sows. Whoever sows to please their flesh, from the flesh will reap destruction; whoever sows to please the Spirit, from the Spirit will reap eternal life. (Gal. 6:7–8)

Statement 2: Feed the spirit. Starve the flesh.

This is the turning point in our battle against the flesh. Whatever we feed grows, and whatever we starve weakens. I don't know about you, but whenever I try to clean up my eating habits and cut out certain foods (like milkshakes from Chick-fil-A), I start craving them, even if I haven't thought about them in months!

Sometimes we are unknowingly empowering the flesh by constantly thinking about it. Instead of trying so hard to *control the flesh*, we need to focus on *strengthening the spirit*.

Maybe you're trying hard to stop being negative with your words. Instead of trying to muster up more self-control to keep your negative words from slipping out, focus on choosing positive things to say and filling your mind and spirit with things that build faith and optimism. Are you struggling with a sense of hopelessness? Take a look at the music you listen to, the movies you watch, the books you read. Start putting in things that fuel hope.

Don't feed the thing you are trying to beat. Weaken the flesh's grip on your life by depriving it of the things that give it strength.

* * * * * *

Every day, you're given twenty-four hours. Within that period, you'll make lots of decisions: how you spend your time, how you spend your money, what you talk about, who you choose to listen to, what attitudes you will cultivate, and what thoughts you will entertain.

Picture two bank accounts—one for our flesh, one for our spirit. If we allow our feelings to rule, we will be making deposits into our flesh. These deposits give it strength. This is what Paul is referring to when he talks about sowing to please the flesh in Galatians 6:8. Here's how it might look in everyday life:

I don't feel like going to work today, so I'm calling in sick . . .

I don't feel like dealing with people today, so I'm going to give them all a piece of my mind . . .

I don't feel like church today, so I'll just sleep in and go to IHOP . . .

I don't feel like exercising today, so I'll just sit here and watch TV . . .

I don't feel like talking about it, so I'll just wait for a better time . . .

When we're sowing to the flesh, our inner conversations and the decisions they lead to revolve around what we *feel* like doing. Sowing to the flesh may seem inconsequential in the moment, but it can sabotage, even ruin, our success if it continues over time.

What might be damaged or even lost if we repeatedly sow to the flesh?

- Good relationships with a spouse, children, friends, bosses, or colleagues
- Success at work
- Opportunities
- Our reputation
- Financial security or material possessions
- Positive emotions such as hope, joy, and peace
- Mental clarity and creativity
- The desire to keep living and moving forward in life
- Health—physical, mental, and spiritual

Perhaps the greatest loss that comes with living by our feelings is a failure to invest in our spiritual growth. When the storms of life hit, we are spiritually bankrupt. We haven't built the spiritual strength we need on the inside to weather the storm. So we run to God in desperate need of a miracle.

Don't get me wrong—God loves to help us, and we should always turn to him in challenging times. But God doesn't intend for us to live crisis to crisis, our spiritual neglect creating a constant need for divine intervention to fix the messes we've created. Instead, he wants us to consistently build strength into our spirit so we are prepared to navigate the storms of life. Maybe it's not a crisis; maybe one day we just wake up and realize we are not where we want to be . . . that there is more to life than what we have made of it.

Sowing to the flesh will never produce what we need to fulfill God's purpose for our life. The reality is, seeds sown to the flesh can only produce negative results. The true purpose, success, and fulfillment God wants us to experience can only be produced by consistently sowing to the spirit.

In his book *Success God's Way*, Dr. Charles Stanley says, "The things you sow in the Spirit are life producing and have the potential for eternal reward. . . . The more you sow to the Spirit, the greater the harvest of things that result in your ability to achieve the goals that God has helped you set."[8] Sowing to the spirit isn't always easy. But we weren't designed to thrive in a life that's easy; we were designed to thrive in a life that's significant.

God is far more interested in helping us achieve his definition of success than ours. Why? Because "success" on our terms will ultimately leave us unfulfilled and discontent. Success God's way is always the best way.

Does it take discipline to sow to the spirit instead of the flesh? Yes. But think about the benefits it can bring: peace, hope, strength, wisdom, good relationships, favor, a healthy body, a sound mind, a strong spirit full of faith, and the list goes on. If we look at the list, who reaps the benefit of seeds sown to the spirit? We do!

It's time to change our inner conversations so they sound a little bit more like this:

> *I don't feel like going to work today, BUT it's the right thing, so I'm doing it . . .*
>
> *I don't feel like being nice today, BUT I'm going to be patient, use kind words, and have a great attitude . . .*

*I don't feel like going to church today, BUT I'm not going to
let my flesh stop me from feeding my soul and spirit . . .*

*I don't feel like exercising today, BUT I know it's making
me healthy, so here I go . . .*

*I don't feel like talking about it because it's an uncomfort-
able subject, BUT we need to figure some things out . . .*

I don't feel like it . . . BUT I'M GOING TO ANYWAY!

Our investments are revealed when a crisis hits. We cannot reap where we have not sown. But by the same token,
we will always reap what we *have* sown. When we've made a
lifestyle of sowing to the spirit, the storms of life may shake
us a little but they won't destroy us. Starving the flesh and
feeding the spirit positions us to thrive in life and beat life's
challenges, instead of life's challenges beating us.

Statement 3: Sow where you want to go.

If we aren't happy with what we're reaping, it's time to
take a look at the seeds we're sowing. A farmer knows that
his harvest is a direct reflection of what was planted in a
previous season. He decides what to plant based on what
he wants to harvest. We need to approach our life the same
way. The choices we make today are like seeds sown into
our future. As we make those decisions we have to remember this: what we *release* determines what we *receive*. We
won't get apples from dandelion seeds. And in the same
way, angry words won't produce peace. Negative attitudes
won't promote a loving environment. Resentment won't
foster relational harmony.

When it comes to moving forward, we have to first get a
vision for a better future. We use that picture in our heart

and mind of where we want to be and then ask ourselves, *What choices do I need to make today to get there?*

Don't let your experiences from the past or the situations in your present determine the choices you make about your future. If you want peace in your marriage, start making investments and decisions to get you there. If it's been characterized by flaring tempers and angry words, more of the same won't move you forward to a place of peace. Don't wait on the other person to "get their act together" or to "deserve" it. Simply start sowing what you would like to receive.

If we want to move forward, we can't make choices based on where things have been—that's called "sowing from our past." We can't sow according to where it is right now—that's "sowing from our present." We look at the future we want and we "sow *toward* our future." Sometimes we need to pause and ask ourselves, *Are the choices I'm making today in alignment with where I want to be tomorrow?*

The great news is, wherever we are, we can start sowing good seeds right now. We might have heard the Chinese proverb that says, "The best time to plant a tree was twenty years ago. The second best time is now." We can't go back and "undo" the poor choices and negative seeds we sowed in our past, but we can stop sowing them and start sowing good ones.

Identifying the "Why" behind the "What"

Our personality, the family we grew up with, our life experiences, the choices we make, the beliefs we hold, and the perspectives we choose (how we see ourselves, God, the world, and so forth) can all influence how we handle our emotions. Whether we realize it or not, our past can have a very powerful effect on our present.

Consider the successful executive who is so driven to succeed he neglects his wife and children. The time he does spend with them, he is tense and easily aggravated. Despite his best intentions, time and time again, angry words spill out. He tells himself his intense efforts to succeed are to give his family a better life, but deep down he can still hear his father's words ringing in his ears—*You'll never amount to anything.* A deep-seated fear of failure is driving his life. Or consider the young woman who is so emotionally fragile she crumbles at the slightest bit of perceived criticism from anyone. A long history of deeply unhealthy relationships have left her feeling she'll never measure up. She is living under the flawed belief she must be perfect in order to deserve love. That skewed belief leaves her constantly striving for approval, desperately hoping to avoid the sting of rejection.

When any kind of brokenness in our soul or spirit goes untreated, it will inevitably produce some type of pain or dysfunction in our life. The mistake a lot of people make is trying to modify the dysfunctional behavior without working through the underlying cause. Some of our emotional hangups are just bad habits we've formed over the years that we need to work on changing, but other emotional challenges are an indication of something deeper that needs to be addressed. Emotional wounds from our past or traumatic experiences can impact us significantly.

If we find ourselves constantly dealing with an unhealthy emotional response or habit, we have to ask ourselves, *Is there a deeper issue causing me to behave this way? Is there an unresolved hurt or a flawed mindset I need to address?* If there are emotional wounds that have gone unresolved, we'll eventually keep going back to that dysfunctional behavior (or replace it with another). The soul's cry for healing will manifest itself in a variety of ways until the wound is healed. Behavior modification will get us only so far. What we really need is heart transformation.

Moving into Love

Often the unhealthy emotional patterns in our life are a response to a painful incident. We form them as a defense mechanism to prevent us from experiencing more pain. These behaviors, no matter how big or small, are rooted in fear. We avoid deep, meaningful relationships because we're afraid of rejection. We strive to be perfect so we won't have to feel the disappointment of letting others down. We don't even try to reach for success because we know the pain of past failures. Allowing fear to create barriers in our life may feel like a safer way to live, but in the end fear will only produce more painful, negative effects.

The great news is change and healing are possible. Renowned psychiatrist Elisabeth Kübler-Ross, MD, observed many people near the end of their lives who carried regret because they realized things could have been different but fear held them back. She makes an interesting observation: "To transcend fear . . . we must move somewhere else emotionally; we must move into love."[9] All the emotions we experience stem from two primary emotions, love and fear. Kübler-Ross goes on to make this powerful statement: "*We cannot feel these two emotions together, at exactly the same time. They're opposites. If we're in fear, we are not in a place of love. When we're in a place of love, we cannot be in a place of fear"*[10] (emphasis added).

This is exactly what 1 John 4:18 tells us: "There is no fear in love; but perfect love casts out fear, because fear involves torment. But he who fears has not been made perfect in love" (NKJV). Maybe you grew up in a harsh environment that has caused you to avoid criticism at any cost. Perhaps there was a lack of affection or approval in your past that has left you endlessly searching for acceptance. Maybe rejection or abuse from a significant person in your life has made it difficult to trust people or form close relationships.

If there are some unhealthy emotional hangups or patterns in your life, I encourage you to spend some time examining your heart for any unresolved hurts or flawed mindsets influencing you. Be willing to dig down into the deepest places of your being. Ask God to reveal what pockets of fear may be hiding in the broken, forgotten corners of your heart. Then let him in, even if the pain is so deep you think you can't.

Letting God into those broken places allows them to come into full contact with his love—his perfect, healing, restoring, freeing love. In order to move forward, we must face the pain of the past (or the present). Fear will always produce and perpetuate pain, but God's perfect love can help us step out of the pain and find true freedom and healing.

You can't change the past, but you can build a healthy future. If progress seems slow, don't get discouraged. Keep sowing good seeds in every season. Being controlled by our emotions can manifest in a lot of different ways. Some emotional hangups require self-discipline and practical lifestyle adjustments; others may require addressing more serious underlying issues or getting professional help. Wherever you find yourself on the journey, don't give up. Hold your course and steady on.

Evaluate / Eliminate / Elevate

Evaluate: Are there areas of your life controlled by your feelings?

Eliminate: What are some changes you could make to "starve the flesh"?

Elevate: What are some practical things you could do to "sow to the spirit" and help yourself move forward?

three

Winning over Worry

Anxiety is an expensive habit.

Max Lucado

Leslie and I have a friend who was a flight attendant for many years. Long after she had changed careers, she started having serious pain in her back and shoulder. It was so bad it was impacting her ability to do everyday things. When she went to get it checked out, they asked her typical questions. Did she do any heavy lifting? Had she experienced any injuries? Was there anything heavy she frequently carried for long periods of time on that side?

She was puzzled at first. She couldn't think of anything that would be causing her pain. It took her a little while to connect the dots, but eventually she realized her pain was in the same arm she had always used to pull her suitcase through the airports during her seventeen-plus years as a flight attendant.

As she pulled the weight of her suitcase behind her, she was unknowingly damaging her back and shoulder. The problem wasn't so much the weight of the small suitcase but rather how she was pulling it. It was putting too much stress on certain muscles and bones. For years they had carried the weight of a load they weren't designed to bear, and eventually that took its toll.

Isn't that a little like some of us, who go through life pulling our worries behind us everywhere we go? Proverbs 12:25 tells us, "Worry weighs a person down" (NLT). When we worry, we are placing unnecessary stress on our mind, our heart, and our body.

Perhaps you've heard the old saying, "It's not the load that breaks you down; it's how you carry it." It's true. We can't stop challenging situations from coming our way, much like our friend couldn't avoid taking a suitcase through the airport for her job. However, we *can* avoid the additional pain and problems that come from worrying about them. Worry is a weight we were never intended to bear.

But what, then, do we do with the challenges life will inevitably bring our way? How do we find peace when the resources at our disposal are no match for the physical, emotional, and financial needs before us? What do we do when we're faced with a problem we don't have control over? A decision that lies in someone else's hands? A child at college, outside of our care and influence? A loved one battling a life-threatening illness? *How do we keep moving forward when the weight of worry feels paralyzing?*

When anxiety threatens to bring our life to a grinding halt, Psalm 55:22 gives us a gentle reminder: "Turn your worries over to the Lord. He will keep you going" (NIrV).

The Age of Anxiety

Everywhere we turn, we're confronted with situations that could be cause for worry. The war on terrorism continues and only seems to escalate. Innocent people are victims of senseless, tragic acts of violence. Natural disasters wreak havoc on tens upon tens of thousands. There are plenty of "big things" to worry about in the world we live in. But studies show our worry and anxiety aren't limited to just the big things—we find little things to worry about every day! Worry is such a huge issue and I've preached on it many times over the years. What I've noticed in my research is that public speaking consistently shows up as most people's number one fear. Death is second. Most people would rather be in the casket than on stage in front of everyone giving the eulogy!

In 1965 Billy Graham, one of the greatest leaders in the Christian faith, wrote, "Historians will probably call our era 'the age of anxiety.' Anxiety is the natural result when our hopes are centered in anything short of God and His will for us."[1] More than fifty years later, these words are truer than ever.

Jesus knew worry would be an issue we would struggle with, and so he took some time to address it. In his famous Sermon on the Mount, Jesus covers some of life's big topics, and it's no surprise worry is one of them.

> That is why I tell you not to worry about everyday life— whether you have enough food and drink, or enough clothes to wear. Isn't life more than food, and your body more than clothing? Look at the birds. They don't plant or harvest or store food in barns, for your heavenly Father feeds them. And aren't you far more valuable to him than they are? Can all your worries add a single moment to your life?

And why worry about your clothing? Look at the lilies of the field and how they grow. They don't work or make their clothing, yet Solomon in all his glory was not dressed as beautifully as they are. And if God cares so wonderfully for wildflowers that are here today and thrown into the fire tomorrow, he will certainly care for you. Why do you have so little faith?

So don't worry about these things, saying, "What will we eat? What will we drink? What will we wear?" These things dominate the thoughts of unbelievers, but your heavenly Father already knows all your needs. Seek the Kingdom of God above all else, and live righteously, and he will give you everything you need.

So don't worry about tomorrow, for tomorrow will bring its own worries. Today's trouble is enough for today. (Matt. 6:25–34 NLT)

In his wisdom and love for us, Jesus is challenging our natural propensity to worry. This word *life* Jesus uses in this passage, in the original Greek, is the word *zoe*. Literally, it means "the fulfillment of life." Jesus isn't talking about the physiological state of being alive with breath in our lungs and a heart beating in our chest. He is referring to the satisfaction of life, the zest of life—the real essence of truly living. When we experience something that resonates deeply with us, or sparks a powerful awakening in the core of our being, we might say it makes us "come alive." *This* is the kind of life Jesus was talking about.

Jesus was saying, "Real life—the fullness of life, the zest of life—isn't found in earthly things." The things we eat or drink or wear can never produce true satisfaction or make us come fully alive—only Jesus can do that.

What's So Wrong with Worry?

Some of us are so used to worrying, it's second nature. Some people would say, "It's just what I do. Is it really a big deal?" The answer is *yes*! Here's why.

Worry puts our focus in the wrong place.

In the Sermon on the Mount, Jesus was trying to get us to step back and take on a more big-picture perspective. Worry distorts our perspective and skews our thinking. When we're looking at life through the filter of worry, we tend to major in the minors and minor in the majors. We start obsessing about things that normally don't bother us. We get frustrated and aggravated over every little thing. When we worry, we start making our problems bigger and God smaller.

God has a great plan for our life, but it's hard to see it when we're looking at life through the filter of worry. It's like trying to use a microscope lens to look at the stars. The stars are there, but we can't see them because we're looking through the wrong filter.

Worry chokes the life of God out of us.

The word *worry* has its origins in the Old English word *wyrgan*, which means "to choke or strangle."[2] It's the picture of an animal attacking its prey. When it attacks, it goes for the throat to strangle its victim. This is exactly what worry does to us too.

Seven chapters after Jesus addresses worry in the Sermon on the Mount, he tells the parable of the sower. It's a story of a farmer who sows his seeds, which fall on four different types of ground. The seed represents the Word of God, and the different types of ground represent the hearts of the people who receive the Word.

One group of people were those who received the seed into thorny ground. Matthew 13:22 tells us the thorny ground represents someone who hears the Word, but the worries of life choke it out and prevent it from producing any fruit. What's interesting is this group of people—those weighed down by the worries of this life—didn't fall away from God. They kept serving him. It was just that the Word of God didn't have any effect in their life. Its power was choked out by their worries and cares. When we think about it that way, we realize worry is pretty much the worst thing we can do when something concerns us, because it cuts us off from the thing we need most: the power of God's Word.

This idea of worry choking the life out of us isn't just metaphorical—it can be quite literal too. When we worry or panic, it can feel like a giant weight is sitting on our chest, squeezing the breath out of our lungs.

Doctors have long agreed about the dangerous effects worry and anxiety can have on our physical and mental health. For example, a twenty-year study conducted by the Harvard School of Public Health found that men who worried had a significantly higher risk of coronary heart disease.[3]

When we worry, it triggers stress chemicals to flood our body. Our body is designed to handle them in short bursts, as they enable us to deal with stressful situations, but we were never intended to have a constant flow of them. When this happens, our body's chemical processes are disrupted and our body can begin to malfunction.

Here are just a few of the conditions linked to chronic worry and anxiety: cardiovascular diseases, headaches, ulcers, hypertension (high blood pressure), irritable bowel syndrome, colitis and Crohn's disease, skin disorders such as psoriasis, eczema, and stress acne, and a decreased immune response, which can lead to even more serious diseases.[4] Unfortunately a lot of people who are wrapped up in worry don't even realize the impact that it's having on their body and mind.

Studies show that 75–90 percent of all visits to primary care physicians are stress-related visits,[5] and people spend $800 million annually on antianxiety medication.[6] Far too many people's lives are at a standstill—or even moving backward—because of the effects of worry.

For some, worry is just a bad habit, a relatively small issue. But there are others whose lives are slowly being destroyed by the suffocating weight of worry. In extreme cases, perpetual mental patterns driven by worry can eventually produce a mental illness.

When we think about it, worry is all about possibilities—but so is faith. Every day we have a choice of how we will see our future. Worry chooses to see the future through the filter of fear. We need to flip our filter and choose to see our future through the filter of faith instead of fear.

Worry can distract us and cause us to doubt God's great plan for our life.

One of my most treasured possessions is a book my father-in-law gave me many years ago. It's an amazing little book by Dale Carnegie called *How to Stop Worrying and Start Living* that was originally published in 1944. Despite its age it's still so good because it addresses worry with timeless truth that is both powerful and practical. It's significant to me not only because of the wisdom in it but also because my father-in-law has been a mentor and a role model in my life in many ways.

One of my favorite stories in it is about a businessman whose life was very close to being destroyed by worry and anxiety. He was in a difficult season of life, having recently closed his private law office and taken a job selling reference books to lawyers. Despite the fact he was thoroughly trained for the job, was well prepared for client meetings, and had significant law experience, he struggled to make sales. No matter how hard he worked, he was unable to make enough to pay his bills. His anxiety mounted as his manager threatened him and his wife begged him for money to buy food for their family.

On one particular business trip, he found himself feeling especially desperate. His sales calls were unsuccessful and he had no money to pay his hotel bill, buy dinner, or even purchase a ticket home. He felt utterly and completely beaten. Distraught and depressed, he began to question if life was still worth living.

In his lowest moment, with nowhere else to turn, he began to pray, asking God to give him understanding and guidance in the midst of the darkness he felt. He poured out his heart, praying he would be able to make sales and have money to provide for his wife and children. As he looked up from his prayer, he noticed a Gideon Bible on the hotel room dresser and began to read it. He described the change that began to take place:

> I opened it and read those beautiful, immortal promises of Jesus that must have inspired countless generations of lonely, worried, and beaten men throughout the ages—a talk that Jesus gave to His disciples about how to keep from worrying:

"Take no thought for your life, what ye shall eat, or what ye shall drink. . . . But seek ye first the kingdom of God, and his righteousness; and all these things shall be added unto you."

As I prayed and as I read those words, a miracle happened: my nervous tension fell away. My anxieties, fears, and worries were transformed into heart-warming courage and hope and triumphant faith. . . . I felt like a new man. And I *was* a new man, because I had a new and victorious mental attitude. . . . My outward situation the next day was the same as it had been through my weeks of failure, but a tremendous thing had happened inside me. I had suddenly become aware of my relationship with God. A mere man alone can easily be defeated, but a man alive with the power of God within him is invincible. I know. I saw it work in my own life.[7]

The next day, he went on with his sales calls. His situation hadn't changed, but he had. Instead of approaching his prospective clients with fear and anxiety, he met them with confidence, enthusiasm, and optimism. He ended the day with more sales than he'd made in weeks. What a dramatic transformation! When we become aware of our relationship with God and the power it makes available to us, it offers us a whole new approach to the situations we're facing.

God's Solution for Worry

There are a lot of great resources to help us learn how to deal with worry, but I encourage each of us to make God's Word the primary one we turn to. In it are some powerful principles that will help us win over worry as we consistently apply them in our life. Let's take a look at two of the most foundational principles: put God first and pursue peace.

Put God first.

As Jesus concludes his teaching on worry in Matthew 6, he gives us a final encouragement to "seek the Kingdom of God above all else" (v. 33 NLT). This is the secret the businessman discovered in that hotel room: putting God first is the starting point for finding freedom from worry.

It's really this simple: when trouble strikes or fear sets in, we're either going to trust God or worry. The choice is ours. Putting God first means we make him bigger than anything else in our life. We elevate him above our wants, our fears, our plans, and yes, our worries. This is the foundation for true peace in our life. Here are some of the ways we put God first:

- **By having a relationship with him.** We admit we're sinners, we ask his forgiveness, and we receive him into our heart as Lord and Savior.
- **By pursuing his kingdom.** His kingdom is his way of doing things. We exchange our way of doing things for his way, and our plans and purposes for his.
- **By taking him at his Word.** This means our heart, our beliefs, our thoughts, and our actions all function as if God's promises are true, even when we can't feel it or see it.

Many of us have heard Jesus's encouragement in Matthew 6:33 to "seek first the kingdom of God and His righteousness," reminding us that when we do, "all these things shall be added to you." The Phillips translation has a freshness that may help this familiar verse resonate with you in a new way: "Set your heart on the kingdom and his goodness, and all these things will come to you."

The thing we set our heart on will determine our desires, our decisions, and ultimately, the direction of our life. When our heart is "set on the kingdom," it keeps us moving forward in the right direction.

Pursue peace.

This is where it gets practical. In Philippians 4, the apostle Paul lays out a pattern for experiencing God's peace in our life. God's peace isn't the product of a trouble-free life; it's the product of holding on to truth in the midst of life's challenges.

Let's look at this simple but powerful pattern for peace:

Don't worry about anything; instead, pray about everything. Tell God what you need, and thank him for all he has done. Then you will experience God's peace, which exceeds anything we can understand. His peace will guard your hearts and minds as you live in Christ Jesus. (vv. 6–7 NLT)

When we break it down, here's what it looks like: don't worry about anything + pray about everything = God's peace will guard our heart and mind. Let's take a look at these action steps.

1. Don't worry about anything.

I know, this is easier said than done. A good first step is to identify our worry patterns. If we can tell when worry starts and its root causes, it's easier to stop. Over the next seven days, try to identify when a worry thought first begins to rise up in your heart. In that moment, stop and try to identify what you are worrying about and why.

Successful people avoid worry by approaching problems in a practical, non-emotional way. Most of them use a thought process similar to this:

1. *What am I worried about?*
2. *Why?*
3. *What can I do about it?*

There is a certain amount of healthy concern we need to have that moves us to be responsible individuals—to pay our bills on time, complete our work, and keep our life in order. But it can quickly cross over into worry. Here's the difference:

Healthy concern: proactive thinking that moves us to responsible action.

Worry: fear-based thinking that doesn't lead to a solution.

How do we know when something has crossed over from healthy concern to worry? When something starts keeping us up at night, affects us emotionally, or causes us to obsess about it—that's when we know we've crossed the line.

One research study had people write their worries for two weeks. Guess what they found? Eighty-five percent of the things people worried about actually had *positive* outcomes, not negative ones.[8] That's incredible! Statistically speaking, we really don't have as much to worry about as we think we do!

Remember the question Jesus asked: "*Can all your worries add a single moment to your life?*" (Matt. 6:27 NLT). Of course not! In fact, if anything, worry will knock a few moments off of it. Here's what we have to remember: *worry doesn't work*. Holocaust survivor Corrie ten Boom said,

"Worry is a cycle of inefficient thoughts whirling around a center of fear."⁹ Worry is our response to problems when faith has been taken out of the equation. We need to replace worrying with a response that actually works: prayer.

2. Pray about everything.

Remember what Paul said: "Don't worry about anything; instead, pray about everything. Tell God what you need, and thank him for all he has done" (Phil. 4:6 NLT). I love it when the Bible gives us "insteads." It just makes it simple. Every time you want to worry, pray instead. Sometimes we overcomplicate prayer, and that keeps us from praying freely, confidently, and frequently. The reality is that prayer is just communicating with God about what is going on in our life.

Paul gives us a very simple formula for what our "instead prayers" should look like: "Tell God what you need, and thank him for all he has done."

Maybe you have a big meeting coming up at work. You're feeling nervous about it because your project—and the possibility of a promotion—are depending on the success of this meeting. You have that unsettled gnawing in your gut, and all those fearful "what-ifs" are popping up in the back of your mind. The moment you start to obsess with worry about your meeting, use it as an alarm to stop and pray.

This is how I pray in these moments: *God, I need this meeting to go well. I need this person to hear me with an open heart and mind. I need to make sure my words make sense and that I connect with the people in the meeting. I need the person on the other side of the table to have mercy on me and give me grace. I'm praying for an A+ meeting. God, I thank you for this job. I thank you I even have a meeting to attend. Thank you that I can trust you, and that you are going to provide what I need.*

Prayer puts the weight of the burden back in God's hands. We can choose to carry the load in a way that God says not to (worrying), or we can roll it back onto God through prayer and let him carry it for us, positioning our heart and mind to receive the protection of peace his Word promises.

Fix Your Thoughts

Worry is born in the mind, so that's where we need to address the problem. We can try a lot of other things to help combat worry, but ultimately, if we don't fix our thinking, we won't stop worrying. Worry happens when we attach our need for security and answers to the wrong things.

Right after Paul gives us the pattern for peace, he offers us one final piece of advice: fix your thoughts on good things (Phil. 4:8). That word *fix* simply means "to anchor something securely." Paul is telling us we need to take our thoughts that are attached to the wrong things and reattach them to the right things.

We've got this area of our house by our back door, right where our kids come in when they get home from school. I don't know how it is in your home, but somehow in our house backpacks seem to always end up on the ground. In two seconds that area can go from neat and orderly to this crazy scene of backpacks, shoes, books, folders, papers, lunch boxes, and water bottles scattered everywhere! When that happens, it gets out of control and it's not functional.

We decided to add some built-in shelves to this specific area so everyone could take their backpack and hang it on a hook to keep everything from getting so out of control. Instead of chaos, things are neat and orderly. It's so much better than backpacks getting tossed to the side and wherever they land is where they stay until the next morning.

Maybe you and I, as mature adults, wouldn't do that with our material possessions, but that's exactly what some of us do with our thoughts. Just like those backpacks, we kind of toss our thoughts anywhere, and wherever they land we just let them stay. When our thoughts aren't fixed on the truth of God's Word, that's when things in our heart and mind start to get chaotic and feel messy. We start to feel out of control, and worry rises up until it feels like it could choke us.

Isaiah 26:3 tells us that God "will keep in perfect peace all who trust in [him], all whose thoughts are fixed on [him]" (NLT). When our mind is fixed on the truth of God's Word, the result is peace in our heart.

For every worry, find a promise in God's Word to address your situation. You might even want to write those verses down and put them on your bathroom mirror or hang them on your refrigerator—whatever it takes to keep them at the forefront of your mind. When worry starts to creep in, anchor your thoughts on that promise and let God fill you with his peace.

Put Your Worry to Work

Worry produces no forward motion. No answers. No solutions. No peace. In fact, worry always has the opposite effect. It drags you backward. Creates confusion. Stirs up doubt and steals your peace. Worry robs you of the tools you need to move forward and accomplish things today. One of the worst things about worry is it can shut down our ability to think clearly and logically, leaving us feeling paralyzed.

Sometimes the solution to peace is as simple as doing something about the thing you're worried about. Are you worried about everything you have to do and afraid it won't all get done? Sit down and make a list of what needs to be done. Next to each task, write how long it will take. Assign a specific time for each task on your calendar. If you can't make them all work, list them in order of priority. Think practically but creatively about how you could solve your problem. Could you ask for help? Reschedule something? Devote your attention to accomplishing the most important items on your list—those that are high priority and time sensitive. If an item must go undone, let it be the low-priority task without a pressing deadline.

Don't be afraid to ask God for help in managing the practical areas of your life. He can give you the wisdom you need to make good choices when you're worried or don't know what to do. Do your part, plan ahead, and do everything you can today to set yourself up for a win tomorrow. But don't let tomorrow steal today's peace.

As Jesus reminded us, tomorrow will have enough worries of its own—troubles you haven't been given the grace for yet. Don't reach into the future and try to handle its problems without the grace tomorrow will bring. Spend today connecting God's grace to what's at hand right now, and trust him to meet you with fresh grace—fresh answers, fresh strength, fresh ideas, fresh provision—for what will be at hand tomorrow.

Evaluate / Eliminate / Elevate

Severe worry or anxiety can be a very serious issue. If you're struggling to make progress in this area, a life-giving Christian counselor can be a valuable resource to help you move forward.

Evaluate: What worries are weighing you down?

Eliminate: Create a practical action step for each worry where possible. For situations you have no control over, pick a specific Bible verse to stand on.

Elevate: Take a moment and talk honestly and plainly with God about the worries listed above. Tell him what you need and thank him for all he has done.

four

So Long, Stinkin' Thinkin'

> The happiness of your life depends
> on the quality of your thoughts;
> therefore guard accordingly.
>
> *Marcus Aurelius*

Several years ago, Leslie and I started to notice a strange smell lingering in the kitchen. Correction—a *terrible* smell. Despite our best efforts, we couldn't figure out what it was or where it was coming from. I searched high and low, exhausting every possible idea I could think of.

I didn't really know what else to do, so I thought maybe—just maybe—it would go away on its own. *Wrong.* Not only did it fail to go away, it got progressively worse.

It became my mission to find and conquer "the smell." I sniffed my way around the kitchen until I was able to identify the general area it was coming from. Oddly enough, it seemed to be coming from one of our wall outlets. I wasn't really sure where my search would take me, but at that point, I was willing to follow any lead to try to put an end to the horrible mystery smell.

I took off the outlet cover, and to my surprise I found a dead mouse. Apparently, it had been running around in the walls, bit into some of the electrical wiring, and made its final resting place in our wall.

Whenever I tell this story, people always chime in with a similar experience. A package of meat fell out of the grocery bag and started to rot under the front seat of the car, or milk spilled on the floor mat and spoiled.

The worst was a story from a sweet young couple with a toddler son from our church. They were moving from Memphis to start a new job in South Carolina, and the husband's company hired movers to pack all their belongings and transport everything to South Carolina.

When they arrived, they got a short-term lease on an apartment and kept most of their belongings in storage while they searched for a home. When they finally found a house many months later, they began to unpack all their boxes from storage, only to find the moving company had packed their trash can still full of trash—*with a dirty diaper in it*. Not the kind of housewarming gift they were hoping for!

Go to the Source

As we were trying to get rid of the smell in the kitchen, we could have lit a great-smelling candle or doused the room with air freshener. It might have provided a temporary fix, but it wouldn't have provided a lasting solution to the problem. We would have had to keep dealing with it over and over again.

Why? Because instead of actually fixing the problem, we would be simply dealing with the symptom. The smell wasn't actually the real problem. The real problem was the dead mouse. In order to get rid of the smell, I had to dig down and deal with it at the source.

Matters of the Heart

In *An Essay Concerning Human Understanding*, British philosopher John Locke said, "I have always thought the actions of men the best interpreters of their thoughts."[1] Basically, Locke was telling us what we *truly* think and believe will ultimately show up in our actions. We might do a really good job of appearing confident, but if we're struggling with insecurity in our thoughts it will eventually begin to show up in our attitudes and actions.

Just like one small dead mouse caused a really undesirable effect in our home, one bad mental habit can produce some really undesirable effects in our life. In order to truly find freedom from the junk holding us back, we're going to have to dig down to the root of the problem: our thinking. Or maybe we should say, *our stinkin' thinkin'!*

Why is our thinking so important? Proverbs 23:7 gives the answer: "For as he thinks in his heart, so is he" (AMP). Our mind is the command center for our life. This verse tells us our thinking determines who we are and the reality we choose to operate from.

I don't know about you, but I've often wondered why the verse refers to a man "thinking" in his heart. Most of us would say thinking takes place in our brain, not our heart. However, science has found the heart has a very complex, independent nervous system all its own.[2] In fact it's even called the "brain in the heart."[3]

In her book *Who Switched Off My Brain?*, Dr. Caroline Leaf talks about the role the heart plays in our life. She says, "Interestingly, though many consider the heart only as the source of love, research shows that the heart considers and 'thinks' about information received from the brain. This implies that the heart has opinions of its own. . . . Your heart is not just a pump. It is your body's strongest biological oscillator, which means it has the ability to pull every other system of the body into its own rhythm."[4]

This is why Proverbs 4:23 instructs us, "Above all else, guard your heart, for everything you do flows from it." Here is how it reads in another translation: "Be careful what you think, because your thoughts run your life" (NCV).

One of my favorite quotes is by James Allen, who said, "You are today where your thoughts have brought you; you will be tomorrow where your thoughts take you."[5] Think about that. Our thinking determines what we *do*. What we do determines our *direction*. Our direction determines our *destiny*. If we want to stay on track with God's purposes and plans for our life, we begin by keeping our thinking on track with his Word.

Capture the _____ Thoughts

When I was growing up, we would go to Wisconsin every summer to visit our extended family. I loved it. My cousins and I would come up with all kinds of games to play, but our favorite was always capture the flag. We would spend hours at night running through the woods, sneaking into "enemy territory" to try to capture their flag. If you captured the enemy flag, you were on your way to victory.

This same tactic is what carries us to victory when it comes to winning the battle in our mind. In 2 Corinthians 10:5 Paul gives us a battle plan for overcoming our stinkin' thinkin' (any thoughts that don't line up with God's truth): "We demolish arguments and every pretension that sets itself up against the knowledge of God, and *we take captive every thought to make it obedient to Christ*" (emphasis added).

This is the foundational process for producing transformation in our life. We touched on this when we talked about worry and Paul's advice in Philippians 4:8 to fix our thoughts on good things. We talked about detaching our thoughts from the wrong things and reattaching them to the right things.

Here are just a few examples of the thoughts we need to capture.

- **Immoral thoughts.** Make a commitment to never entertain any thought that would lead you away from a place of strength and purity—no matter how small. In his devotional *Faith Alone*, based on Martin Luther's doctrine of justification by faith, James C. Galvin offers advice for how to deal with these kinds of thoughts: "You should follow the advice of a hermit who was approached by a young man complaining of having lustful thoughts and other temptations. The old man told him, 'You can't stop the birds from flying over your head, but only let them fly. Don't let them nest in your hair.'"[6]

- **Negative thoughts.** Negativity is one of the most common types of thinking that keeps people from moving forward in life. A negative attitude can make people critical, full of doubt, pessimistic, fearful, or just plain apathetic. They figure nothing good can happen to them, so why even try? You may think being negative isn't a big deal, but the truth is, negativity is rooted in fear, and fear is not of God. It just doesn't produce anything good in our life! In fact, scientists have found thoughts rooted in fear and the negative emotions that stem from fear generate toxic chemicals and cause damage to the brain if they are produced consistently.[7]

It's easy to see that the word *negative* is close to the word *negate*, which means "to cause to be ineffective or invalid." How many times have we caused good things in our life to be ineffective or invalid because we failed to have the confident expectation God tells us to have? As Joyce Meyer says, "We can't have a negative mind and a positive life."[8]

I'm challenging you to a little experiment: commit to "capture and quit" any negative thought that comes in your mind for the next seven days. Don't entertain it in the least. Instead, flip it. Find something positive. Hope for the best. Expect something good. If the only change we made was to commit to stop thinking negative thoughts and exchange negative thought patterns for optimistic, faith-filled ones, I think many of us would experience drastic change. Baseball Hall of Famer Wade Boggs said, "A positive attitude causes a chain reaction of positive thoughts, events and outcomes. It is a catalyst and it sparks extraordinary results."[9] Once you start to "capture and quit" the negative thoughts in your mind, you just might be surprised at the difference it can make!

- **"Mistaken identity" thoughts.** When the devil wants to keep a person down in life, one of his most successful strategies is to lie to them about *their identity* and *God's identity*. In the chapter on emotions, we talked about how our life experiences can shape our thinking. What we believe to be true about ourselves, others, God, and life is shaped through the filter of those mindsets. The problem is, those mindsets may reflect what we have experienced but that doesn't mean they reflect the truth. Far too many people think of God as cruel, demanding, unloving, and distant. But if we read Scripture, we see God is gracious (Ps. 145:8), loves us unconditionally (Rom. 8:38), and wants to be close to us (Ps. 145:18).

  Or maybe we're plagued by thoughts such as, *I'm such a failure . . . I'm worthless . . . God couldn't really love someone like me.* The truth is God's Word says we are his masterpiece (Eph. 2:10), we are valuable (1 Cor. 7:23), and we are loved with an everlasting love (Jer. 31:3). But if we don't know the truth, we continue to operate from the reality of the lie.

  We have to get good at filtering our "mistaken identity" thoughts that don't line up with what the Bible says. It's not easy. Some of you may have "mistaken identity" thoughts that have been in your mind as long as you can remember. It may have never occurred to you that some of the ways you think about yourself, God, or life in general may not be rooted in the truth.

  The best way to start capturing and quitting mistaken identity thoughts is to spend time reading the Bible and finding out who God is and what he says about us. From this we can gain a true understanding about our identity in Christ, which is essential for a healthy, secure, thriving life. As we replace our flawed thoughts with the truth of God's Word, we begin to experience inner transformation and freedom.

Knowing the truth about who God is and who he says you are will be the foundation of true freedom. Capture any thought that doesn't line up with God's Word and replace it with the truth.

Willpower and Warfare

The reality is, whatever controls our mind controls our life. I love the promise God gives us in 2 Timothy 1:7: "For God has not given us a spirit of fear, but of power and of love and of a sound mind" (NKJV). A sound mind is strong, healthy, peaceful, and able to make good decisions. It means we are able to think clearly and maneuver wisely through situations. We can handle transitions and problems well. We can navigate life without being overtaken by confusion, chaos, or emotions. A sound mind enables us to make Spirit-led, wise decisions that will move our life forward.

Maybe your mind and thoughts aren't in a place of health and strength like God's Word says they can be. If that's the case, I want to encourage you: change is possible. The key is to "let God transform you . . . by changing the way you think" (Rom. 12:2 NLT). Most of the issues that hold us back in life can be traced back to unhealthy thoughts or mindsets. Bad habits, insecurity, negative patterns in relationships—and the list goes on. If we want to fix the issue, we have to fix the thinking that drives it.

We all know mental habits can be hard to break. Have you ever been driving down the road on your way to work and suddenly realized you were supposed to be going to the store—in the opposite direction? Your mind had gone on autopilot and you ended up going somewhere you were *used* to going, not where you were *supposed to be* going. Maybe you've even felt like a mental habit or thought pattern was ingrained in your mind—as it turns out, it actually is. The thoughts we think repeatedly literally wear grooves into our brain so we can function more efficiently. The longer we've thought a certain way, the easier it is physically for our brain to think that old thought rather than form a new one, because the pathway is already there. To change our thoughts we have to create new pathways—to literally wear new paths into our brain and bypass the old ones. This typically takes about twenty-one days.[10]

Renewing our mind and overcoming our stinkin' thinkin' is about more than just forming new thought patterns in our brain. Ephesians 4:23 tells us, "be constantly renewed in the spirit of your mind [having a fresh mental and spiritual attitude]" (AMP-CE). This shows us two keys to renewing our mind and changing the way we think:

- A fresh *mental* attitude—WILLPOWER
- A fresh *spiritual* attitude—WARFARE

We have to make the decision to change and then discipline ourselves to make choices that will produce the new habits we want in our life (willpower). But we also have to realize the battle for our mind and our thinking is a spiritual one—one the enemy does not want us to win. He will do whatever he can to keep us trapped in thinking contrary to

God's Word. This is a battle that needs to be fought with spiritual weapons (warfare).

It comes back to a simple equation I talk about all the time: *God's part/my part*. It's easy to lean too far one way or the other. For some people, achieving change is all about exerting self-discipline and sheer willpower. For other people, it's all about miraculous deliverance received from God. What I have found is it's usually somewhere in the middle. Even when we see someone receiving a miracle in the Bible, that person brought something to the table—even if it was simply faith, boldness, or humility.

Here's how we have to approach it as we work to renew our mind: *My part is to do everything I can do to position myself so God can do his part.* **God's part is his presence. My part is my position.**

When I was a single young man trying to win Leslie over, you better believe I went to great lengths to put myself in her presence. Not only did I want to be near her, but I was completely convinced that if we spent some time together she would realize I was the man of her dreams!

We need to have that same kind of persistence and tenacity when it comes to experiencing God's presence. God is the essence of everything we need to become whole. As we repeatedly experience him, we are changed to become more like him.

Some of you may have grown up in an unhealthy home, and your thoughts are a complete mess. Others of you have just spent years not paying much attention to your thoughts and you've collected some "stinkin' thinkin'" along the way. No matter what you may be facing, know that there is no mindset, thinking pattern, or stronghold in the mind that is beyond the power of God.

Painted with the Power of the Spirit

Isaiah 10:27 says, "It shall come to pass in that day that his burden will be taken away from your shoulder, and his yoke from your neck, and the yoke will be destroyed because of the anointing" (NKJV). *Yoke* and *anointing* aren't words we really use today, but the anointing is as life-changing as ever. The yoke Isaiah is talking about is the old-fashioned kind where a heavy wooden bar rests over the shoulders of two oxen and is fastened under their necks by a metal collar.

In the Bible, the yoke represents bondage—being tied to something that limits freedom. When those oxen are bound together under the yoke, virtually all their freedom has been taken away. They are powerless to remove the yoke themselves. It must be removed by an outside force. For you and me, the outside force that removes the yoke of bondage in our life is the anointing—God's presence. The word *anointing* is *chrisma* in the original Greek. It's very closely related to the word used in the New Testament when the gifts of the Spirit are talked about, which is *charisma*. The word *anointing* literally means "to be painted with the power of the Spirit."

When we put this back together, we see this verse is saying: *the strongholds in our life will be destroyed because of the power and presence of God*. That means we need to do everything we can to experience the anointing in our life. Let's look at three powerful weapons that help us do spiritual warfare and experience the anointing—the power and presence of God.

1. God's Word

God's Word is the ultimate tool for transformation in our life. John Stott said, "We must allow the Word of God to confront us, to disturb our security, to undermine our complacency and to overthrow our patterns of thought and behavior."[11] God's Word may force us out of our comfort zone. It may confront some issues in our life and challenge some unhealthy thoughts in our mind. Honestly, it may not be what we want to hear, but it is the truth that will set us free (John 8:32).

The Bible is so powerful because it gives us tangible words—*God's words*—to replace the tired, anxious, depressed, or any other unhealthy type of words polluting our mind. The more we fill our mind with the Word of God, the less room there is for thinking that can hold us back. As God's Word gets stronger in our mind, the grip of those toxic thoughts grows weaker and weaker until it is broken.

God's Word has so many incredible qualities and effects on our life. It not only teaches us about God but also cleanses and purifies us, provides direction, brings peace, removes fear, produces wisdom, instructs and corrects us, encourages us, strengthens us, and the list goes on and on. But there is one effect in particular I want to highlight because it sums up the impact God's Word has on our life. We see it in both Joshua 1 and Psalm 1.

> Keep this Book of the Law always on your lips; meditate on it day and night, so that you may be careful to do everything written in it. Then you will be prosperous and successful. (Josh 1:8)

> > Blessed is the one who . . . meditates on his law day and night.
> > That person is like a tree planted by streams of water, which yields its fruit in season

and whose leaf does not wither—
whatever they do prospers. (Ps. 1:1–3)

In Joshua we see the words *prosperous* and *successful*, and Psalm 1 uses the word *prospers*. The same root Hebrew word is used in both verses: *tsalach*. *Tsalach* means "to cause to prosper; to advance; to make progress; to be profitable; to cause to succeed." In these verses, the word *prosper* is referring to the effect God's Word has on our life.

We could say it this way: *God's Word causes us to prosper, to advance, to make progress, to be profitable, and to succeed.* We have to be proactive in getting God's Word into our heart and mind. God's Word can't produce benefits in our life if it's not in our heart and mind. No one else can do this for us!

Here are five things we can do with God's Word:

1. Hear it.
2. Read it.
3. Meditate on it.
4. Memorize it.
5. Speak it.

Charles Spurgeon is said to have quipped about John Bunyan, author of *Pilgrim's Progress*: "If you cut him, he'd bleed scripture."[12] That's a goal we should all strive for. When God's Word is consistently present in our thoughts, our life will grow progressively stronger and healthier. It will keep us moving forward in every season, even the difficult ones that cut us to the core and cause us pain. Whatever we have put in is what pours out.

My wife had an amazing mom. When Leslie and I were dating, I'd go to pick her up and her mom would insist on feeding me every time—usually I'd have eaten an entire meal by the time Leslie came out from the back. Leslie's mom was a wonderful cook and an incredible host. And while we appreciated those things, what we loved most about her was her wisdom, strength, and kindness—she was a woman of integrity and character.

We always imagined her in our life when we pictured our future. But one October, we got the kind of news everyone dreads. Leslie's mom had cancer, and suddenly our future drastically changed. Two months later she was gone.

It was one of the most difficult seasons we've known as a family, and I would say the most difficult season Leslie had ever walked through. In that time of grief and dealing with the loss of her mom, Leslie had some CDs in her car. One of them was a teaching series she had from a great friend of ours, Nancy Alcorn.

Nancy is the founder of an amazing ministry called Mercy Multiplied. For over thirty years, Nancy has been building homes for girls with life-controlling issues where they can heal and rebuild their lives. When she teaches, almost everything coming out of her mouth is Scripture. (I think she may bleed Scripture, too, if you cut her!) Everything they do at Mercy is rooted in God's Word, focused on getting truth into these girls. The transformation it produces is amazing.

Leslie credits those CDs in her car with keeping her on track during that season. The Word of God washing over her heart and mind guarded her from getting pulled off course or caught in an unhealthy place during an extremely painful time. There's nothing like God's Word to heal us from our past, guide us in the present, and prepare us for the future.

2. Prayer

Prayer is our lifeline to the power and presence of God. Abraham Lincoln dealt with a significant amount of difficulty in his life. He lost his mother at a young age, endured countless failures in politics, and suffered the death of his eleven-year-old son while steering our nation through one of the most tumultuous periods in its history. He once said, "I have been driven many times upon my knees by the overwhelming conviction that I had nowhere else to go. My own wisdom and [the wisdom of those around] me seemed insufficient for that day."[13] Prayer doesn't always take away the challenges we are facing, but it does bring God into the middle of them. In the fight to change our mind, it's an essential—and effective—weapon.

Scientific research has shown that twelve minutes of focused prayer every day for eight weeks can produce enough change in the mind to be measured on a brain scan.[14] While toxic thoughts like fear, anxiety, and unforgiveness can damage the brain and body through the chemicals they produce, when we pray our body produces chemicals that have a positive effect. These chemicals heal the damage and create physical changes the brain and body need to thrive.[15] Fear and anxiety will never change anything, but prayer does. It can change our situation—but perhaps even more importantly, it changes *us*.

Fasting is a great companion to our prayer life from time to time, especially if we're in need of a breakthrough. Fasting is simply saying no to some appetite in our life (especially food) to create an increased hunger for the things of God. Fasting doesn't bring change in and of itself but rather positions us to experience the anointing, which will bring change into our life.

3. A Life-Giving Church Environment

Next to the Word of God, the local church has been the single most influential force in my life. A life-giving local church is one of the key ways God connects us to the things we need to overcome and thrive in life. One of my favorite verses is Psalm 92:13: "Planted in the house of the LORD, they will flourish in the courts of our God." Our life is like a seed and the church is like soil. As we plant ourselves and "put down roots" into a healthy local church, we are able to draw out all the "nutrients" to nourish our life and help us grow. Here are some of the things we experience in a healthy, life-giving church:

- **Worship.** Psalm 22:3 tells us God inhabits our praise. This means worship brings the presence of God into our life! I highly encourage you to make worship a part of your individual time with God each day, and also commit to worshiping with other believers in a local church (Heb. 10:25).

- **Teaching of God's Word.** When we hear God's Word, it helps us grow more mature as Christians and get to know God better. It encourages our spirit, strengthens us, and equips us for the challenges we face.

- **Relationships.** Psalm 68:6 says, "God sets the lonely in families." His house is a place where you can belong and be a part of a family. Healthy, godly relationships enrich our life, bring joy and encouragement, and help us through tough times. They're also important because much of the work God wants to do in us takes place in the context of relationships. We can learn new things, grow as a person, and develop our character.

- **The Holy Spirit.** Nothing can replace an environment where the Holy Spirit is valued and embraced. The Holy Spirit brings a kind of life and power that can't be found from anything else. He comforts, guides, corrects, and gives us the power we need to live the way God has called us to live.

I could fill an entire book with stories of people whose lives have been changed by getting planted in God's house. Let me share just one of them, from an incredible young man in our church, in his own words.

> The very first time I came to The Life Church was when I was in middle school. One of my friends had invited me so I thought, why not? I went for a little while but ended up leaving and not going to church for a long time. It was during these years that I went through some dark seasons in my life, struggling with depression, insecurity, drugs, and alcohol, and I had just lost hope for myself. My freshman year of high school, my friend who had invited me to church that first time saw what my life looked like and he knew it wasn't looking good. He invited me back a few times before I finally agreed to go. But when I walked into church that Wednesday night, I had no idea I would be leaving as a saved Christian. I remember the message was about opening up your heart to God and if you just give him a mustard seed–sized amount of faith, then he can move mountains with it. So I decided to let God into my heart and he rescued me from the life I was living. He gave me hope, friends and purpose. And since then I've started serving in church. . . . As I write this, I look back on my life and see how greatly I have changed. . . . Psalm 107:14: "He brought them out of darkness, the utter darkness, and broke away their chains."[16]

Evaluate / Eliminate / Elevate

Renewing our mind and clearing out the stinkin' thinkin' holding us back from God's best is both a battle and a process. Stay in the fight and allow God to give you a new mental and spiritual attitude to help you move forward with a new level of freedom.

Evaluate: What areas of your thinking might qualify as "stinkin' thinkin'"?

Eliminate: What unhealthy thoughts do you need to capture?

Elevate: What truth from God's Word do you need to focus on in place of that captured thought?

Writing down a list of Scripture or Scripture-based statements and reading it daily is great way to "rewire" our thought patterns and replace unhealthy thoughts with God's truth.

five

Time to Press Reset

It is never too late to start over.

Rick Warren

Peanuts creator Charles M. Schulz said, "All you need is love. But a little chocolate now and then doesn't hurt."[1] Especially if it's in the form of Reese's peanut butter cups. I love those things . . . *a lot*. Especially the little mini ones. Somehow Reese's peanut butter cups seem to make it into every message I preach. They are my weakness. And I can always find a way to justify them. *They have protein from the peanut butter . . . I think?*

Sometimes I'm on the way home and I'll stop to get gas, and before I know it I've got a king-sized package of them in my hand. I tell myself, *I'll just eat one and save the other two for tomorrow.* Two minutes later they're gone. Leslie has joked more than once that I might have a problem.

Unfortunately, peanut butter cups aren't my only weakness when it comes to food. One summer, I went to preach at a church in Connecticut and decided to stay in New York City overnight on our way there. Our hotel was near an amazing place called the Shake Shack. They should have some kind of advisory posted for people like me who have compulsive eating habits, because they have the best burgers and fries I've ever had, bar none. And their milkshakes. I really can't put into words what those shakes are like . . . I think one time I described them to someone as "life changing" and "a spiritual experience." They are crazy good. So good, in fact, that on my twenty-four-hour stop in NYC there may or may not have been six to eight peanut butter shakes consumed between me and one other guy traveling with me.

What?! Those shakes are crazy good, but . . . that's just plain crazy! On the way home, I had this terrible feeling in my gut—and not from all the shakes I'd eaten. It was the feeling you have when you've given in to something you knew you shouldn't have . . . again. That sinking feeling you have when you know God's been dealing with you about something but you're kind of trying to pretend he isn't.

This was an area I was really struggling with. I would wrestle with it on a daily basis. First Corinthians 9:25 tells us that to be successful in this journey of walking with God, we need to be disciplined and self-controlled in all things. When it came to my food and my physical life, I wasn't even close.

I would try to do well and not give in to my old habits. I'd do ok one day, but then the next day I'd cave and be back at the gas station picking up my king-size pack of Reese's peanut butter cups and spicy nacho Doritos again.

You may be thinking, *Hold up. I don't really think a few too many shakes or some peanut butter cups and Doritos are really that big of a deal. It's not like they're a sin.* And you're right—there's nothing wrong with enjoying food and splurging now and then. But it was an area where I wouldn't—*couldn't*—say no to myself when I needed to.

So there I was, in a season of wrestling with this issue, and one day God dropped something in my heart I will never forget. As clear and as loving and as positive and as forgiving as I have ever heard, he said, *John, this area of your life is out of control. It's beyond my reach. You have taken it away from my reach. It's time to press reset.*

Are You Mastered?

That experience was a wake-up call. I realized I couldn't pretend it wasn't a big deal anymore. I got very intentional about my health, educating myself and putting my new knowledge into practice. I was amazed at the difference it made. Not just physically—I sensed a difference spiritually too.

As long as I resisted God's leading to change, it seemed like there were some other areas I just couldn't quite get traction on—the momentum wasn't there. When I finally surrendered and obeyed, it was amazing how some of those things I had been praying and believing for began to change. I truly believe my obedience opened a door to my breakthrough. Sometimes, when we're feeling stuck in a holding pattern, wishing God would move in our life, it just might be he's waiting for us to follow through on the last thing he asked us to do!

God's influence in our life is usually proportionate to our level of surrender and obedience. My real issue was less about junk food and more about the fact there was an area in my life where I was keeping God at arm's length. The truth is, it had me mastered. Romans 6:12–14 cautions us,

> Therefore do not let sin reign in your mortal body so that you obey its evil desires. Do not offer any part of yourself to sin as an instrument of wickedness, but rather offer yourselves to God as those who have been brought from death to life; and offer every part of yourself to him as an instrument of righteousness. For sin shall no longer be your master.

Sometimes we justify things in our life—like king-sized peanut butter cups and peanut butter milkshakes. Or unhealthy relationships, or what we watch late at night. We tell ourselves, *It's not hurting anybody . . . so-and-so does it . . . I could be doing something much worse.* But the reality is that any area of our life not fully submitted and within reach of the Holy Spirit will create a roadblock.

The junk in our life slowing us down isn't always sin. In Hebrews 12:1, Paul encourages us to "strip off anything that slows us down or holds us back" (TLB). What this means is the standard for evaluating habits in our life is no longer just, *Is this wrong?* but instead, *Is this holding me back or controlling me?*

James 4:17 reminds us, "it is sin to know what you ought to do and then not do it" (NLT). This opens our eyes to a different definition of sin—a definition we need. If there is something in your life that God begins to deal with you about, don't delay in obeying. Sometimes it's the "big stuff" that has us mastered—a drinking problem, viewing pornography, or another destructive habit. But sometimes it's the "little stuff" like eating habits, time management, or disorganization that is stealing our momentum in life. Anything that has us mastered will not only slow us down from moving forward but, if it goes unchecked, will also eventually cause us to start moving backward.

The Downward Spiral

Several years ago I preached a message series on freedom. Our church put up a website where people could anonymously request prayer for issues in their lives they were too ashamed to talk about but desperately needed freedom from. My heart broke for the number of people whose lives were being destroyed by secrets and strongholds they couldn't escape.

One prayer request in particular caught my attention, because so many people have a similar story:

> I never thought I'd be the one that would get so caught up in drugs, especially cocaine. I was the girl that always had it all. The summer after my freshman year of college I went through a bad breakup and lost it and resorted to drugs to make me happy . . . they did for a short time until everything started falling apart.

Research has found that substance abuse causes more deaths, illnesses, and disabilities than any other preventable health problem in the United States today. It is estimated that between thirteen and sixteen *million* people are in need of substance abuse treatment.[2] Most people don't just wake up one day and go looking for an addiction or destructive habit to ruin their lives. A lot of times the strongholds that end up destroying people's lives start out as small, even innocent responses to some kind of pain or emptiness.

First Peter 5:8 tells us the devil prowls around like a lion looking for someone to devour. His schemes for destruction start with him roaming around our life, looking for any opportunities or any areas of weakness where he can work his way in. When Satan tempted Jesus in the wilderness and failed, Scripture says he "left him until a more opportune time" (Luke 4:13 AMP).

An opportune time is simply a time when we are vulnerable; our defenses are down and we might compromise.

There are four opportune times we need to be aware of:

1. Unmet expectations
2. Unreasonable adversity
3. Unexpected temptation
4. Unfulfilled obedience

If the devil can capitalize on an opportune time, he can gain a foothold in our life, and if he gets a foothold, it can turn into a stronghold. When the enemy gets a foothold in our life, it is the first step in what I call "The Spiral of Destruction," which has five stages altogether.

Stage 1: The enemy gains a foothold.

Any place in your life that is out of sync with God's principles is a potential entry point for the devil's scheme of destruction. So many people's lives are destroyed by something that started out innocently. A text, an email, a legitimately needed prescription. But somewhere along the way, in a moment of weakness, you give in and cross the line. You start pushing boundaries and say, "I'm just going to do it once," or "Just one more time." Before you know it, you're losing control.

Stage 2: You begin to try to quit, but you fail and start feeling hopeless.

You feel like a failure, which only increases the anxiety and pain. As a result, you actually start embracing the habit, substance, or stronghold even deeper, turning to it for comfort. At this phase, you are dealing with shame and self-loathing. You start to buy in to lies from the enemy, usually about your identity and worth: *I'm such a failure, I'll never beat this . . . I've already screwed everything up anyway, I may as well give in . . . God must hate me for being like this.*

Stage 3: Any threat to your habit becomes a threat to you.

At this point you start to protect your habit, and a sense of denial sets in. You're struggling and someone you love says, "I'm worried about you," or "I think you have a problem." You get defensive, maybe even angry, and that person becomes your enemy. Many times, you start going to greater lengths to hide your problem and/or distance yourself from people who might confront you.

Stage 4: Your habit becomes a part of your identity.

Have you noticed how we talk about addiction? We say, "I'm an alcoholic. . . . She's a gambler. . . . He's a smoker." We create labels for ourselves and others based on our issues. Satan's goal is to get you to personalize your addiction and make it a part of who you are. He wants you to be wrapped up to the point where you can't separate the addiction you have from the person you are. He wants you to make your addiction your identity.

Sometimes we accept our issue as just part of who we are—we have resigned ourselves to that identity. If we have an eating problem, we make jokes about it to kind of break the tension. I want to encourage you not to give up or settle for a life defined by a certain issue or struggle. Your issue is not your identity.

It's crucial we separate who we are in Christ from whatever it is we may be battling. Instead of making alcoholism part of your identity and saying, "I'm an alcoholic," I think it's better to say, "I'm a child of God and I'm struggling with alcohol." We say, "I'm a child of God" first because that's who we are first. What you do does not define who you are.

Think positive and speak positive. Don't confess negative things over your life, even jokingly, because our words have influence. Even if you've dealt with something your entire life, by the power of God, you can change!

Stage 5: You begin to lose friends, family, money, and/or health, which further wounds your struggling self-esteem.

You feel even worse about yourself and you just ease the pain with the next fix. Many times the more you lose, the deeper the addiction goes. The deeper it goes, the more you lose. Life starts to unravel. Maybe it's gotten to the point where you can't keep a job. Your relationships are crumbling and you're running through money so fast to support your habit. If it progresses, you can reach a point where you are in danger of literally losing everything. If you find yourself at this fifth stage, you are in a precarious position and you need to reach out for some support and help to keep things from imploding.

The truth is, this is where the enemy wants to bring us. His goal is always to steal and kill and destroy. What he wants more than anything else is to disrupt God's mission here on earth. If he can get us distracted, addicted, or locked into a negative habit, he knows he can keep us from fulfilling God's mission and the divine assignments attached to our life.

Understanding the enemy's goals and our own vulnerabilities can help us outwit the devil's schemes to derail us. I can't stress enough the value of using wisdom and staying obedient to God's Word, even in the "little things." It can save us so much heartache and keep us on track with God's plan for our life.

The Tipping Point

So what do we do if we find ourselves trapped in a habit or a way of living that is less than God's best? I want to say this clearly: if you find yourself in over your head, you may need to get professional counseling. There is no shame in seeking out the help you need. There are some amazing, life-giving professionals who can help you walk through the freedom and healing process. I also encourage you to really take hold of and implement the keys to changing our thinking we talked about in chapter 4: prayer and fasting, God's Word, and a Spirit-filled church environment.

Breaking free from life-controlling issues isn't easy. I would never want to minimize your struggle or sound simplistic in any advice I give. However, I do believe these three simple "starter steps" can help you begin to move toward freedom.

1. **Admit the truth.** John 8:32 tells us the truth will set us free. We have to stop making excuses and blaming other people for the state we are in. Admitting it is the first step

to quitting it. We can't fix a problem we won't admit to having. Go to God and admit you have a problem and need his help. He already knows, so don't be ashamed to come to him. Confession is powerful. The Bible tells us when we confess our sin, God forgives us and cleanses us from all unrighteousness (1 John 1:9). We are the ones who benefit from admitting our struggles to God. I'd also recommend admitting your struggles to the appropriate people in your life. What grows in the dark dies in the light. Bringing your struggle into the light is the first step to freedom.

2. **Quit the habit.** If there is something or someone who leads you to the addiction, the thing mastering you, cut the ties—completely. If you have a person who is your supplier or your tempter, disconnect from the relationship. Effective immediately. No exceptions. No contact. They are not a friend to your future. If you keep sinning sexually with the same person, tell them it's over, then delete their number! No texting. No emails. No hooking up. No hanging out. Ever. Do you view pornography? Block the websites you visit, and download an app that tracks you and sends a report to a trusted friend who will keep you accountable. You need to make the choice to be done with that way of living. Do whatever it takes to cut the ties. Yes, it may feel extreme, but your future is worth it. Your future *depends* on it.

3. **Submit your life.** *Submit* simply means "to yield." This is part of God's prescription for success. The Bible gives us two key ways we submit our life. James 4:7 tells us, "Submit yourselves, then, to God. Resist the devil, and he will flee from you." Ephesians 5:21 then tells us to

"submit to one another out of reverence for Christ." First there is a "vertical submission" where we submit our life to Christ and we're yielded to the things of God. This means we obey God's Word and deal with issues he leads us to change. But then there is a "horizontal submission" where we have people in our life who have entrance into our world. We have intentionally opened our life to certain people and have given them permission to get in our business and give us the uncomfortable truth when we need it. The chances of avoiding the Spiral of Destruction go up dramatically when we are yielding our life to a trusted, healthy group of people.

Shame off You

Many times, when people fall into a habit or a destructive lifestyle, they pull away from God, from church, and from Christians because they are afraid they will be humiliated and rejected. Unfortunately, there can be so much shame attached to life-controlling issues, especially in the Christian world.

But if we look at John 8:1–11, we see an amazing story. It shows Jesus's heart toward us when we are trapped in an unhealthy way of living. Jesus was coming to the temple early in the morning, getting ready to teach, when the Pharisees and the instructors of the law came in, dragging a woman who was caught in the act of adultery. They wanted to trap Jesus and find something they could use against him. If he said she should be let go, they would say he disregarded the law. If he upheld the law, which called for stoning, he would have caused an uproar over her death.

Instead of playing into their hands, Jesus bent down and wrote in the dust. There are several theories about what it was Jesus wrote. Many people believe it might have been the sins of the men who were accusing this woman. What we do know for sure is it completely changed the atmosphere in just a moment's time. When Jesus stood up from writing in the dust, he turned to the crowd and said, "Let the one who has never sinned throw the first stone!" One by one her accusers walked away. Finally, it was just the two of them left. As Augustine said, "The two were left alone, the wretched woman and Mercy."[3]

And then Jesus said those amazing words: "*Neither do I condemn you. . . .* Go now and leave your life of sin" (John 8:11, emphasis added). The lesson here is this: *religion rejects. Jesus restores.*

In the lowest moment of her life, when she would have been filled with shame and humiliation, Jesus showed her love, grace, and mercy and offered her a new lease on life—the chance to press reset. *Just like he does for you and me.*

This story sums up the heart of God toward those who are entangled in a life of something they need to leave behind. He is not angry with you. He loves you. He hasn't given up on you. *But he is calling you to something better.*

Three small, simple words from Jesus show us what our next steps are:

"Go."

This is an action word. Someone once said two-thirds of God's name is *go*. Go simply means to start moving. To start taking steps forward. For us, it means it's time to press the reset button and step into a new season.

I would imagine, for this woman, that moment of standing there before Jesus and all those men would have been the lowest point in her life. But it also became the turning point. Our lowest points have the opportunity to become turning points—*if they propel us to action.*

Sometimes we think destructive effects only come into our life through actions, but the truth is sometimes we are not where we want to be in life because we have *not* acted—we have not done what it takes to get there. President John F. Kennedy said, "There are risks and costs to action. But they are far less than the long range risks of comfortable inaction."[4]

You have to step out of something old before you can step into something new. Jesus stepped into the adulterous woman's world so she could step out of it. Instead of focusing on her past, he pointed her in the direction of her future. He told her to shake off the shame and step forward. She was guilty, but she was not condemned. She was free to *go.* And so are you.

"Now."

This is about timing. We've heard the saying, "Timing is everything." It's especially true here. We must go *now*. Not tomorrow, not next week, not next year. Not when the subscription runs out, when we finish our stash or reach the end of the bottle. Not when the finances are better or the kids go off to college. The time is now.

The key is creating the shortest response time possible. We must make the changes we know we need to make right now, without waiting another day.

"For God says, 'At just the right time, I heard you. On the day of salvation, I helped you.' Indeed, the 'right time' is now. *Today is the day of salvation*" (2 Cor. 6:2 NLT, emphasis added). The word *salvation* simply means "to be rescued." The word picture given in the original Greek is to be snatched out of a flame. The implication is that time is of the essence. Would you wait around until tomorrow if you were trapped in a burning house? I doubt it. Don't wait to step out toward freedom.

There is only one choice standing between us and the start of a new season: the choice to change. No one else can make that choice for us. We have to make it for ourselves. Legendary basketball coach John Wooden said, "Failure is not fatal, but failure to change might be."[5] One choice could change the rest of our life for the better.

"Leave."

Forgiveness comes with a call. It comes with some responsibility. Jesus said, "Leave your life of sin." He forgave the woman's sin but he also called her to step out of it. Forgiveness is a call to step out of sin and into something better. An invitation to step out of our current situation and into a new season.

It's true that whenever we ask, God forgives—no matter how many times we need forgiveness! That's amazing and powerful. But as great as God's forgiveness is, what he really wants to give us is freedom. God's grace makes it possible for us to actually *step out* of a way of life. We don't have to just be forgiven—we can be free!

God's grace gives us the power to walk away from anything holding us back. Grace is God's divine empowerment to be who he's called us to be and do what he's called us to do. There is a gap between who we are and who God has called us to be, but we don't have to try to close that gap on our own. Grace is what helps us get to the place God wants us to be. Again, I can't overstate the power of the "God's part/ my part" principle when it comes to overcoming the habits and strongholds in our life.

The path leading us away from the things holding us back will not always be easy, and change won't happen overnight. Anything worth having comes with a price. But the price of freedom is always less than the cost of addiction or life-controlling issues.

Our old habits and hangups don't have to run our life. Jesus "gave his life to purchase freedom for everyone" (1 Tim. 2:6 NLT). There is so much hope in that. In his great love for us, God is reaching out and offering each of us the chance to step forward into freedom today.

Evaluate / Eliminate / Elevate

Evaluate: Is there an area of your life where you need to press reset? (An insecurity, a habit, a relationship?)

Eliminate: Is there anything in your life that has you mastered?

If you're struggling with an unhealthy habit or addictive behavior, here's a little quiz to help you find out if it's got you mastered:

1. Do your family and friends think you have a problem?
2. Do you continue even though you're hurting yourself or other people?
3. Do you arrange your schedule around it?
4. Can you go a week without it?
5. Is it leading you to isolation?
6. Are you trying to keep it a secret?

If you answered "yes" to three or more, it's likely you're mastered. If you are, take the steps you need to begin your freedom journey.

Elevate: What is one practical step you need to take to start the "reset" process?

(Sadly, some people get so mastered they give up completely. Too many lives are lost as a result of addiction, depression, and suicide. The weight of their burden gets so heavy, they don't see the point of going on or don't feel like they are able to go on. If that's you, please don't suffer alone. Speak up and reach out for help. Even if the present and past have been extremely painful, God can help you move forward and find hope again.)

six

Restricted Access

Get mad, then get over it.

Colin Powell

I grew up with three older sisters who loved to torment me. When we were growing up, one of the things they knew would rile me up was to get into my room. I was in an enviable position because as the only boy I had my own room. They worked together to devise this plan where one sister would lure me out of my room, and then another one would run into my room, slam the door, lock it, and start going through all of my stuff. It drove me crazy!

After a while, I wised up and discovered the secret to beating their scheme. As soon as I knew the trick was on, I would sprint back to my room, and before my sister could close the door, I'd stick my foot in the doorjamb.

No matter how hard she slammed, there was no way she could get my door closed with my foot in it. Sure, it might have hurt a little bit, but with a shoe on, the foot is pretty tough. I knew forcing my way back into my room didn't take much. All I had to do was get my foot in the door.

That's exactly how the enemy tries to use anger in our life. Ephesians 4:26–27 warns us, "'In your anger do not sin': Do not let the sun go down while you are still angry, and do not give the devil a foothold." Some people assume all anger is wrong, but this passage shows us it's possible to be angry and still not sin. Anger, in and of itself, is not sinful—it's what it *leads us to* that can be sinful.

When we look at Scripture, we see there are two kinds of anger, sanctified anger and sinful anger. Sanctified anger is when we get angry about something that angers the heart of God and do something good about it. Sinful anger is when we get angry about something that doesn't matter, or it does matter but our anger leads us to act in a way we shouldn't.

Sanctified Anger

When we get angry about the right things, anger can actually be a powerful force for good. Martin Luther said, "When I am angry, I can pray well and preach well."[1] History has been written largely by people whose righteous anger and action created turning points that significantly changed the future. Even Jesus got angry, and we know he never sinned. In Mark 3:4–5 we see a great example of sanctified, or righteous, anger as Jesus confronts the Pharisees who hoped to accuse him of healing on the Sabbath:

> Then Jesus asked them, "Which is lawful on the Sabbath: to do good or to do evil, to save life or to kill?" But they remained silent.

He looked around at them in anger and, deeply distressed at their stubborn hearts, said to the man, "Stretch out your hand." He stretched it out, and his hand was completely restored.

Jesus's anger propelled him to confront a problem and then do something good to fix it. If we aren't getting a little angry at some negative things—especially the areas of our life that are beneath God's best—then we're probably complacent. Complacency is one of the enemy's most successful strategies to keep people from thriving and moving forward in life. If the enemy can keep us complacent, he can keep us from accomplishing our kingdom purpose in life.

Complacency starves our calling because it keeps us from pursuing the very things we need to grow and thrive. When we're complacent, our God-given talents atrophy within us and the opportunities designed to move us forward go untouched.

We think the enemy will try to get us significantly off track by luring us into some deep sin. In reality, he's more than happy to let us stay on the right track but make us so complacent we never completely step into the fullness of the calling on our life.

This story about Jesus shows us it's ok to get angry. In fact, some of us *need* to get angry. Is your marriage suffering? Is an unhealthy relationship hindering your walk with God? Are issues from your past sabotaging your future? Then you might need to get a little angry. Not at your spouse. Not at yourself. Not at people who have hurt you. You need to get angry at the enemy who is trying to undercut your strength, health, and success with his schemes.

Sanctified anger can spark a "rise up moment" in our life where we say, *Enough is enough. I'm making a change.* It can produce a turning point that compels us to fight for the vision and calling that's on our life.

Sinful Anger

Notice Paul says, "Do not let the sun go down while you are still angry, and do not give the devil a foothold" (Eph. 4:26–27). Anger becomes a problem when it goes unresolved. In the original Greek, the word *foothold* means "room."[2] What makes unresolved anger so dangerous is it opens an emotional door to the rooms of our heart.

Just like my foot allowed me to gain entrance back into my bedroom, anger is the "foot" in the doorjamb that holds the door open for the enemy to gain entrance into our life. Proverbs 25:28 puts it this way: "If you cannot control your anger, you are as helpless as a city without walls, open to attack" (GNT).

When sinful anger controls us, we are allowing the enemy to position us for self-destruction, because sinful anger almost always leads to bad decisions. Harsh words that cut deep. Rash decisions that bring regret. Emotional judgments that are made on feelings rather than facts. A split second of anger can produce decisions that we regret for a lifetime.

Spewers versus Stewers

Most of us deal with anger in one of two ways: we "stew" or we "spew."

Spewers are the people who express their anger and just let it all out. When they're angry, you know it. They blow up in a volcanic eruption that spews toxic emotions and words all over everyone. Spewers tend to feel better right away and move on because they got it all out, but everyone in their path is left burnt to a crisp, struggling to recover from their scathing emotional and verbal outburst. Proverbs 29:11 reminds us, "A fool vents all his feelings, but a wise man holds them back" (NKJV).

Stewers, on the other hand, are people who hold it all in and bottle everything up inside. They might look self-controlled on the outside, but below the surface they're seething. They are rehashing every detail, planning their response, and formulating their argument. Stewers tend to have a harder time moving on after a fight because they're keeping it all alive inside as if it happened yesterday. Their anger can last for years. Psalm 32:3 says, "When I kept silent, my bones wasted away through my groaning all day long."

Spewing and stewing are both dangerous habits because they are the result of giving in to our flesh. Spewers need to discipline themselves to filter their initial responses and cool off before they speak or act. Stewers need to learn how to communicate openly and honestly instead of keeping it all inside.

The High Price of Anger

Bottling up anger and other negative emotions inside us is extremely harmful emotionally, relationally, physically, and spiritually. When we experience anger, it creates a series of chemical reactions that physically affect our body. The chemical by-products of anger are toxic if they are produced perpetually. Consistent anger literally poisons us from the inside out.

Dr. John Barefoot conducted a twenty-five-year follow-up study of 255 medical students that revealed the individuals who scored highest in hostility on personality tests were almost five times more likely to die due to heart disease than classmates who were less hostile. The study also revealed they were seven times more likely to die by the time they were fifty years old.[3]

When the Bible gives us instructions to guard our heart, to forgive, or to deal with anger quickly, it's for our own good. Not only for the sake of our spiritual health, but for the sake of physical and emotional health too. Even the best modern medicine for our bodies can't fix a problem in our soul.

In his book *Deadly Emotions*, Dr. Don Colbert describes one specific example of this. He explains how toxic emotions such as anger, rage, and bitterness are interpreted by the body as stress. When stress is constant, the immune system goes into overdrive, as if the throttle were stuck in high gear at all times. The immune system not only attacks bacteria, viruses, parasites, fungi, and cancer cells but also healthy cells, eventually resulting in an inflammatory autoimmune disease such as rheumatoid arthritis or lupus.

He shares the story of a middle-aged woman named Lois who came to his office hoping to find relief from the mild arthritis pain she had in her fingers. He prescribed a common anti-inflammatory for her pain, which provided some improvement for a while, but soon her condition worsened. Blood tests confirmed Lois had rheumatoid arthritis, and she was referred to a rheumatologist for more specialized care.

As a part of her initial physical exam, Dr. Colbert asked Lois about her personal history. She revealed she was in a difficult, stressful time in her life, coming out of a messy divorce. After thirty years of marriage, her husband decided to leave her for a much younger woman. In the blink of an eye, everything in Lois's life changed for the worse. Her marriage was over and she was alone. Instead of a sprawling mansion and a fancy car, she now had a tiny apartment and a not-so-nice used automobile. Lois had once enjoyed a very wealthy lifestyle, but now she could hardly make ends meet.

Dr. Colbert recalled the unexpected bitterness and anger that came pouring out when Lois began to talk about the divorce:

> Just at the mention of her former husband's name, Lois's soft, sweet countenance and gentle manner changed dramatically. Her face became contorted into a snarl. With deep anger in her low, nearly whispery voice, she told me that she hated her husband and wished him dead. The more she talked, the more her eyes seemed to become smaller and her glare more defiant. She was actually smiling as she told me how much she wanted him to die—and not a peaceful death, either. She wanted him to lose his life painfully and to experience even greater suffering than she had. Rarely had I encountered such deep bitterness and resentment in a patient . . .
>
> Certainly, Lois had plenty of reasons to be bitter. But reasons do not produce bitterness. Attitudes do . . .
>
> Regardless of what the specialist prescribed, Lois's condition only grew worse as the months and years went by.[4]

Proverbs 14:30 tells us, "A calm and undisturbed mind and heart are the life and health of the body, but envy, jealousy, and wrath are like rottenness of the bones" (AMP-CE). Unfortunately, a lot of people handle their anger the same way as Lois and live with painful emotional and physical consequences. Of course, not every disease is caused by negative emotions, but it would be foolish to ignore what both the Bible and science confirm: the issues in our heart and mind directly impact our physical body.

The Action Plan

You may be thinking, *Yeah, this is great and all, but what should I actually do when I feel mad?*

I'll be honest, there have been times I fired off a hasty reply to a heated email or said the first sharp response that came to mind in an argument. I've failed in this area, and I'm learning action in the midst of untempered emotion usually leads to regret. Here's a little pattern to help us keep a level head and make good decisions, even in the midst of heated emotions.

1. Freeze

Pause before you act—even for just a split second. There's an old Chinese saying: "If you are patient in one moment of anger, you will escape a hundred days of sorrow." When Abraham Lincoln felt his emotions rising up and was tempted to communicate with someone in an emotionally charged way, he would write what he referred to as a "hot letter." He'd freely vent his frustration and anger into a letter and then put it aside. After he'd cooled off, he'd go back to the letter and write on it: "Never sent. Never signed." Thanks to this wise practice, General George G. Meade never had to read the letter that put the weight of Lincoln's blame on him for Robert E. Lee's escape after Gettysburg.[5] Hit the pause button first to avoid charging headlong down the wrong path.

2. Filter

The ancient Roman poet Horace said, "Anger is brief madness." And it really is true—anger can make us do all kinds of crazy, insane things we wouldn't normally do! Logic and reason are the first things to go when we get angry. We need to force ourselves to slow down and filter our thoughts logically and rationally to avoid making knee-jerk emotional judgments we'll regret later, asking ourselves, *Is this really worth another second of my time? Does this matter in the grand scheme of life, or am I pursuing a foolish emotional release?* It's always helpful to try to see it from the other person's point of view. We must make a habit of filtering our thoughts in light of the big picture before we turn them into words or actions.

3. Fight

You're probably thinking, *Wait—isn't fighting something we're supposed to avoid?* Actually, when our anger rises up on the inside, even after we freeze for a moment and filter our thoughts and emotions, we're still probably going to have a fight on our hands. We just have to choose the right fight.

There are really two choices when we get angry. We drop it and move on, or we address the issue. Both will require a "fight"—just not the same kind. Dropping it usually requires a fight within ourselves, battling the temptation to let unhealthy, angry thoughts and emotions control us. Or, if the issue needs some resolution, we need to choose to "fight fair" and engage in healthy interaction aimed at resolving the issue. The key words are *fight fair*! Conflict is inevitable, but it doesn't have to be damaging or devastating. It can actually produce healthy growth if handled properly.

Fighting Fair

There's a little piece of advice Leslie and I always try to remember, and it's one I always pass on to young married couples: sometimes the best thing to do is *just don't say it*. When you're in the middle of a "discussion," there is always a moment when you know you could drop the issue and just let it go—or you could jump on it and start ranting. Learn to discern where the line is and don't give in to the flesh's desire to cross it. "Starting a quarrel is like breaching a dam; *so drop the matter before a dispute breaks out*" (Prov. 17:14, emphasis added). We don't have to take the bait for every "anger opportunity" that comes our way.

Sometimes, though, we bump up against issues that legitimately need to be discussed and worked through. If you do need to talk things out, make sure you set up some guidelines to keep the fight healthy and fair.

1. **Find the right time.** If you need to talk about something, don't just unload it whenever you feel like it. Use wisdom in picking the right time. Some times to avoid:
   - *Tired times.* Don't start a fight when one—or both—of you are tired and at your worst (late at night, right after a long day, and so forth).
   - *In the heat of the moment.* Take a cooling off period before diving in. This helps you settle your emotions so you can communicate clearly and logically.
   - *Over text or email.* If at all possible, always try to handle conflict in a face-to-face conversation.
2. **Watch your words.** Groucho Marx is said to have quipped, "If you speak when angry, you'll make the best speech you'll ever regret." Angry words are easy to say, but it's hard to undo the damage they can cause. They are like seeds that get implanted in people's hearts.

   The truth is, you can build someone up even in a difficult

situation. Stay away from absolutes and over-exaggeration such as "always" and "never." Be humble and apologize quickly. Most importantly, don't just say whatever pops into your mind. "A gentle answer deflects anger, but harsh words make tempers flare" (Prov. 15:1 NLT).

Tips for hard conversations:

- Don't rip the other person's head off when they are honest with you.
- Don't be so fragile they can't talk to you because they're afraid you'll fall apart.
- Don't blow it off or shut down. Be brave enough to have the tough conversations.

3. **Keep resolution the goal.** We need to "fight forward" and engage in healthy, conflict-resolving dialogue. The goal should always be aimed at making progress, achieving peace, and improving the health of the relationship or situation. We don't fight to "win" or to seek an outlet for heated emotions. Sometimes you have to agree to disagree and decide to pick it back up at another time. But sometimes the best thing to do is give grace—to not be overly sensitive and give people a little room to be human and make mistakes.

As we discipline ourselves to process our anger in a healthy way, we get better and better at making good choices in the midst of emotionally charged situations. This can save us a lot of heartache and regret.

A Root of Anger

Everyone gets angry now and then. It's normal. But if you are perpetually struggling with underlying anger, or if your anger frequently escalates to rage, there may be a deeper issue to address. This is what we could call "a root of anger."

Sometimes an anger problem isn't so much a *self-control* problem as it is a *pain* problem. Most serious anger issues stem from an inner wound that has not healed. Abuse of any kind, rejection, traumatic childhood experiences, death of a loved one, loss of a significant relationship, a parent with an addiction, neglect, and severe poverty are just a few of the experiences that can produce deep-seated anger.

This deep-seated anger can also produce other emotional issues such as perfectionism, a need to control, self-doubt and low self-worth, cynicism and criticism, promiscuity, and "bursting" emotions (a sudden emotional reaction that is more intense than what a normal response should be).[6]

When anger is repressed instead of resolved, it can continue to impact our life in very real ways. It can sabotage relationships, make it difficult to keep a job, and even impact our health. And yet, as painful as the consequences of anger are in our own lives, the reality is we are not the only people our issues affect. Anger can deeply hurt the people in our life—especially spouses and children. It's never ok to hurt or abuse people—physically, verbally, or mentally. If you're even close to that point, you need to stop, ask for forgiveness, and get help.

Most of all, you need to deal with the root. Often the solution to an anger problem is not managing angry behavior more effectively but rather finding healing for unresolved hurts and wounds. English novelist Edward G. Bulwer-Lytton said, "Anger ventilated often hurries toward forgiveness; and concealed often hardens into revenge."[7] Dealing with the root may mean taking a step you have never taken before. Maybe it's admitting the hurt and pain something from your past caused you. Grieving a loss that left you angry and hurting. Releasing a desire for revenge. Letting go of blame.

If you think back to Lois's story, she let one event define the rest of her life. She allowed one extremely painful tragedy—her divorce—to create another: a life of hostility and bitterness. By choosing to remain angry, she robbed herself of any enjoyment she could have had in her final years.

Closing the Door on Anger

If anger has been a significant struggle in your life, don't wait another day to begin addressing it. I encourage you to follow these three steps:

1. **Admit the hurt.** Acknowledging our pain is the first step for receiving healing. If we refuse to acknowledge a wound, or if we keep it at arm's length from God, it's very difficult for it to heal.
2. **Ask for help.** Ask God to heal the wound and help you release the anger and bitterness. Many people find meeting with a godly, life-giving counselor for a season can help them better navigate the healing process.
3. **Surrender it all.** We hold on to anger sometimes because we feel we have the "right" to. But ultimately we don't, because God says not to let it go unresolved. Letting go of anger requires a good deal of dying to self—humbling yourself, swallowing your pride, and choosing God's way over your way. It's not easy, but it can change your life.

Don't let the enemy have easy access into your life through unhealthy anger. Remember, whatever you are angry about, sinful anger can't make it better. When you surrender and choose to let go of anger, God can help you move forward, heal your heart, and bring restoration into your life.

Evaluate / Eliminate / Elevate

Evaluate: Are there situations in your past or present you are angry or resentful about? Even if you don't think there are, take a minute and examine your heart, asking God to show you any places there might be hidden anger or resentment.

Eliminate: Are there any unhealthy habits you have when it comes to dealing with anger or conflict (spewing, stewing, and so forth)?

Elevate: What is one practical action step you can take to start handling anger in a healthier, more God-honoring way?

seven

Unlock the Door (and Throw Away the Key)

Life is an adventure in forgiveness.

Norman Cousins

Nelson Mandela's greatest hope was to see South Africa become a place where all people could "live together in harmony and with equal opportunities." In 1964, he was imprisoned for resisting apartheid (meaning "apartness"), and he remained there for twenty-seven years. When he was finally released he had spent more than a third of his life incarcerated. During that time, his mother and one of his sons died, and he was not allowed to attend either funeral.[1] Despite the difficulty and injustice he endured, when he spoke about his time in prison he stated, "As I walked out the door toward the gate that would lead to my freedom, I knew if I didn't leave my bitterness and hatred behind, I'd still be in prison."[2]

Prison. It's the perfect description of what unforgiveness does to our life. In fact, this is the exact picture painted for us in Proverbs 18:19: "An offended friend is harder to win back than a fortified city. Arguments separate friends like a gate locked with bars" (NLT). We're going to draw out three phrases from this verse to help us understand the devastation of unforgiveness and then unpack some truths to help us guard against it.

Here's the first phrase: *an offended friend*.

Truth #1: Unforgiveness will keep you locked in.

One of the words the Bible uses for *offense* is the Greek word *skandalon*. It paints the picture of the trigger of an animal trap where the bait is placed.[3] When an animal is out hunting, it's enticed by the lure of the bait. If it falls for the trick and takes the bait, the trap door slams shut, locking the unsuspecting animal inside.

This is the picture of what happens when we hold offense or unforgiveness in our heart. This is so important to understand in the context of trying to move forward in life, because unforgiveness always has the opposite effect. Unforgiveness traps us in the moments when we have been hurt the most, turning us into a prisoner of our past. It acts like a chain around our heart, constantly connecting us back to that person or situation that hurt us. As much as we may want to move forward, we can't. The unforgiveness we carry toward those hurtful situations is the very thing that keeps us tethered to those hurtful situations.

The Bad Seed

I've noticed this little pattern when something hurtful happens in my life, and I think it's true for most of us. Something takes place that causes us pain. Hurtful words from a loved one. Betrayal from a friend. Abuse from someone you trusted. That hurt is like a seed that gets planted into the soil of our life. If we don't deal with it immediately and pull that seed out by forgiving and releasing the person who hurt us, it stays buried in our heart.

As we hold on to these things and replay them over and over in our mind, we're setting the seed a little deeper into the soil. We're watering it and giving it fertilizer. After a little while, it puts down roots and a sprout starts to appear. Over time it grows larger and larger and begins to take up more and more space in the garden of our life. Before we know it, the seed of hurt has grown into what the Bible calls a "root of bitterness" (Heb. 12:15 NLT).

My friend, can I share a little bit of really honest truth with you? Bitterness is not very attractive. A bitter person is often angry, defensive, easily offended, and negative. They usually have an underlying mentality that someone else should pay for the unhappiness they're experiencing. These kinds of attitudes will drive people away and cause us to miss out on a lot of opportunities and blessings in life. If you're struggling with bitterness, my heart isn't to offend you but rather to flash a warning sign that I hope could keep you from further heartache and pain.

We may think our bitterness only impacts one area of our life, but nothing could be further from the truth. It actually impacts every part of our life because it's rooted in the very core of our being. If we let bitterness keep growing, it becomes the filter we see the whole world through. Our life starts to be defined by that situation and the pain it caused us. Eventually we become a prisoner of our own bitterness.

Choosing to forgive is fighting a battle for the freedom of our heart. It won't be easy. But it's a battle we need to fight. The truth is, we don't forgive for the other person; we forgive for our sake and for the sake of the future God has for us.

The movie *Invictus* depicts the challenges that Nelson Mandela fought as he worked to bring integration to South Africa after he was released from prison. There is one scene in the movie that I especially love. Mandela wants to integrate his security forces but is met with opposition from his men. He replies, "Forgiveness liberates the soul; it removes fear. That's why it's such a powerful weapon."[4] Forgiveness doesn't set the other person free—it sets *us* free.

Locked Up

Let's add the second phrase: an offended friend *is harder to win back*.

Truth #2: Unforgiveness will keep you locked up.

The New International Version puts it this way: an offended friend is "more unyielding than a fortified city" (Prov. 18:19). The word *unyielding* means "not soft, rigid, not open, inflexible." To be more unyielding than a fortified city is to be closed off with walls up on every side, nothing coming in and nothing going out.

So many people who are harboring unforgiveness have hardened their heart. This isn't just a metaphorical expression; the stress of negative emotions we carry can actually produce a buildup of plaque that causes the heart to become physically hard, even to the point where it feels like stone during an autopsy.

When we get hurt, the temptation is to lock ourselves behind walls to protect ourselves from getting hurt again. But the problem is those walls keep the old hurts in and they keep good things out—things like healthy friendships, new seasons, new opportunities, and even the conviction and encouragement of the Holy Spirit we all need.

The truth is, we cannot afford to live with unforgiveness. It's far too high a price to pay. It will hurt us emotionally. It will hurt us spiritually. It will even hurt us physically.

Do you remember Lois? Sadly, her disease progressed, as did the bitterness and resentment she carried. Over time, her fingers and toes became deformed and her back and neck twisted into a terrible position. Knowing the effects ongoing emotional stress could have on the body, Dr. Colbert began to suspect that the condition of Lois's mind and emotions and the condition of her body might have been connected. Lois passed away angry and filled with hatred toward everything and everyone in her life. After her death, Dr. Colbert reflected on the unfortunate effect of Lois's choice to withhold forgiveness:

> Today, I am firmly convinced that bitterness and unforgiveness may actually have caused Lois's arthritis. Had she made the very difficult choice to forgive her former husband, she may have prevented the devastating pain and suffering that accompanied her physical condition. In the end, her resentment did not hurt her former husband or his new wife nearly as much as they had hurt her . . . literally in both her body

and her soul. . . . A relative informed me that she had died in near paralysis—her body had become a prison filled with both physical and emotional pain.[5]

Lois is a sad but all-too-common example of the damage and destruction unforgiveness can bring into our life. Her unyielding heart left the flow of forgiveness stagnant, neither giving nor receiving it. The result was she was locked up in her painful way of living, shutting out any possibility of change and happiness.

Time to Give Up

We get our word *forgive* from a combination of two Old English words that came together to create the meaning "to give up completely." Eventually it grew to carry the idea *to completely give up the desire or power to punish*.[6]

I think Paul knew what a struggle it can be to let things go, so in Ephesians he lays out a very specific list of what we are to give up: "Let all bitterness and wrath and anger and clamor [perpetual animosity, resentment, strife, fault-finding] and slander be put away from you, along with every kind of malice [all spitefulness, verbal abuse, malevolence]" (4:31 AMP). He continues by giving us what we are to do instead: "Be kind and helpful to one another, tender-hearted [compassionate, understanding], forgiving one another [readily and freely], just as God in Christ also forgave you" (v. 32 AMP).

The truth is, as Christians, the basis of our faith—everything we've been given by God's grace—comes through the forgiveness he offers us. It's what sets the pattern for how we are to forgive others.

How does God forgive?

1. He forgives *instantly*.
2. He forgives *completely*.
3. He forgives *freely*.

Let me ask you: *Have you received God's forgiveness?*

The truth is, most of the world is dying to hear those three words, "You are forgiven." The weight of guilt is a paralyzing burden to live with. When Jesus came, he came with an incredible offer—to forgive us and lift the weight of our guilt and shame. First John 1:9 tells us, "If we confess our sins, he is faithful and just and will forgive us our sins and purify us from all unrighteousness." This was a verse I memorized when I was a new believer, and I'm so thankful I did, because it set me free from the weight of guilt and the burden of thinking God was constantly holding my sins against me.

A lot of people walk around with a cloud of guilt and condemnation hovering over them all the time because they don't feel forgiven or accepted by God. When we feel guilty and unforgiven, we tend to withhold forgiveness and put guilt and condemnation on others too. It's very hard to give others what we don't have ourselves.

On the other hand, when we get a revelation of how great God's forgiveness toward us is, and how much we've been forgiven, it's so much easier to extend compassion and forgiveness to others. No matter what we have done, God can and will forgive us.

Don't let a hardened, unyielding heart stop the flow of forgiveness in your life. Embrace the forgiveness God has given you so you can let it flow to others in the same way: instantly, completely, and freely.

Locked Out

Here's the third key phrase: an offended friend is harder to win back *than a fortified city*. Arguments separate friends like a gate locked with bars.

Truth #3: Unforgiveness will keep you locked out.

In Luke 15, we read the famous story about the prodigal son. It's a tale of a wealthy family whose sons were privileged enough to have a sizable trust waiting for them, most likely upon their father's death. But the younger son brazenly demanded his portion early and hit the streets to enjoy his new fortune. Not unlike some of the stories we hear about today, right?

What happens next is a pretty familiar turn of events as well. The cash runs out, the new "friends" move on, and he goes from A-list to D-list overnight. He finds himself at rock bottom, eating pigs' food to stay alive, desperately considering his options.

Full of regret and humiliated, he returns home, hoping the father he insulted might accept him as a servant. But instead of rejection, he's met with a welcome he never could have imagined. Not only is he forgiven, he is *celebrated*.

The father and the younger son are usually in the spotlight, the focus of a joyful reunion that displays forgiveness and restoration. However, there's another little subplot happening that sometimes gets overlooked. In the midst of what might have been the happiest moment of his father's life, the elder brother was brooding and backpedaling his way out of the celebration.

"The older brother became angry and refused to go in" (v. 28). Wow. Think about it . . . *he refused to go in*. Instead of feeling the joy and love that should have been present in the moment, he found himself experiencing feelings of anger and resentment.

Unforgiveness produces a distorted perspective. In this case, it distorted the older brother's perspective to the point where he saw something good for his family as something negative for him personally. It caused him to interpret the situation through the unhealthy filter of unforgiveness and all the emotions that come with it—anger, frustration, comparison, and jealousy.

As a result, he made poor choices in his relationships, building a barrier between himself and those he loved. He locked himself out of all the good his father had intended for him to be part of. He was so concerned with things being fair, he couldn't forgive. He got so hung up on restitution, he missed out on reconciliation.

Has unforgiveness locked you out of something great God wants to do in your life? Let me tell you, friend, the long-term cost of unforgiveness is never worth the short-term "satisfaction" we think it will bring. The one who will suffer most is you. Unforgiveness keeps the pain alive in our heart and mind. But even more devastating than the pain it causes is the disruption it creates in our relationship with God.

Many of us know the Lord's Prayer—the famous passage in Matthew 6 when Jesus teaches his disciples how to pray. Not only does Jesus teach us that forgiveness should be a regular part of how we approach God in prayer but just a few verses later he gives yet another strong call to forgiveness: "In prayer there is a connection between what God does and what you do. You can't get forgiveness from God, for instance, without also forgiving others. If you refuse to do your part, you cut yourself off from God's part" (Matt. 6:14–15 MSG).

Still Learning to Forgive

You might have heard of an incredible woman named Corrie ten Boom. Corrie and her family were Dutch Christians who were committed to helping Jews escape being killed by Nazis during World War II. Corrie and several of her family members were arrested for their involvement and sent to a concentration camp. Several of them, including Corrie's beloved father and her sister Betsie, died.

Years later, in an article called, "I'm Still Learning to Forgive," Corrie shares a poignant moment when she was forced to confront the pain of her past. She had just finished giving a talk on forgiveness in the basement of a church in Munich when she saw a man making his way toward her. As soon as she laid eyes on him, she was transported to another time. The man standing before her was a heavyset man in a gray overcoat and brown felt hat. But in her mind she saw him dressed in a blue uniform with a skull-and-crossbones-emblazoned cap on his head—the uniform worn by the guards at Ravensbrück concentration camp.

Yes, there was no doubt—this man had been one of the guards. The sight of him sparked a flood of memories from that horrible chapter of her past: the harsh prison conditions; the humiliation of walking past him naked; the image of Betsie's dangerously frail, exposed body. Anger welled up fresh at the thought of Betsie's death and the unspeakable atrocities they had endured in the concentration camp. As far as Corrie was concerned, he was complicit.

And now there he stood in front of her, hand extended, complimenting her on the message she had just shared. A message about the beauty and power of forgiveness, describing how God throws our sins into the deepest waters never to be brought up again. A message she had compelled others to embrace—yet she herself struggled to embrace it when faced with the same decision. Would she forgive? *Could* she forgive?

The man went on to tell her how he'd become a Christian, how he knew God had offered him forgiveness for the terrible things he had done, how he hoped that she would too. Her blood seemed to freeze and more images from the past flooded her mind. She fumbled in her purse rather than take his extended hand. Could he really think it was that simple? That with one simple request he could be forgiven for the unspeakable suffering he had caused her and countless others? She recalled the inner war that took place in that moment:

> It could not have been many seconds that he stood there—hand held out—but to me it seemed hours as I wrestled with the most difficult thing I had ever had to do.
>
> For I had to do it—I knew that. The message that God forgives has a prior condition: that we forgive those who have injured us. "If you do not forgive men their trespasses," Jesus says, "neither will your Father in heaven forgive your trespasses."
>
> I knew it not only as a commandment of God, but as a daily experience. Since the end of the war I had had a home in Holland for victims of Nazi brutality. Those who were able to forgive their former enemies were able also to return to the outside world and rebuild their lives, no matter what the physical scars. Those who nursed their bitterness remained invalids. It was as simple and as horrible as that.

And still I stood there with the coldness clutching my heart. But forgiveness is not an emotion—I knew that too. Forgiveness is an act of the will, and the will can function regardless of the temperature of the heart. . . . "Help!" I prayed silently. "I can lift my hand. I can do that much. You supply the feeling."

And so woodenly, mechanically, I thrust my hand into the one stretched out to me. And as I did, an incredible thing took place. The current started in my shoulder, raced down my arm, sprang into our joined hands. And then this healing warmth seemed to flood my whole being, bringing tears to my eyes.

"I forgive you, brother!" I cried. "With all my heart!"

For a long moment we grasped each other's hands, the former guard and the former prisoner. I had never known God's love so intensely, as I did then."[7]

When our heart is wounded at the hands of others, forgiveness can feel impossible. Corrie experienced the same temptation the older son did in the parable—to stay angry, to back away from the one who had caused such pain, to punish and withhold forgiveness from one who was undeserving.

But unlike that son, Corrie made the decision to take a step—the only step she could—toward offering forgiveness. It was there, in the little she could offer, that God met her and did the unthinkable: he unlocked her heart in a way she could not and made complete forgiveness possible.

I know some of you have been so deeply hurt and wounded by others that you've wondered if you could ever recover. But I also know that in the face of even the most excruciating hurt and injustice, God can give you the strength and grace to forgive the people who hurt you. Even when it feels impossible.

Start with the step right in front of you. Even if all you can do is whisper a silent cry for help and force yourself to make the smallest gesture of forgiveness, just as Corrie did, start there. God will meet you. Even if you are still learning to forgive.

Breaking Down the Barrier

Forgiveness can be so painful because it forces us to reexperience the deepest hurts we've buried in our heart. Don't shy away from the process of releasing forgiveness because you're afraid of the pain. It is painful because it needs to be dealt with. Dealing with it, while painful, is part of the process of healing. The pain is an indicator you are truly getting to the core of the wound and are on the right path to freeing yourself and moving forward.

If you are struggling with feelings of hatred toward someone who has wronged you, let me gently encourage you to consider these wise words from Dr. Martin Luther King Jr.: "There is nothing more tragic than to see an individual whose heart is filled with hate. . . . Hate destroys the very structure of the personality of the hater. . . . Never hate, because it ends up in tragic, neurotic responses."[8]

Dr. King lived a life filled with opportunity to harbor hate and unforgiveness, and yet he chose forgiveness because he understood the power it holds. He said:

> We must develop and maintain the capacity to forgive. He who is devoid of the power to forgive is devoid of the power to love. . . . Forgiveness does not mean ignoring what has been done or putting a false label on an evil act. It means, rather, that the evil act no longer remains as a barrier to the

relationship. Forgiveness is a catalyst creating the atmosphere necessary for a fresh start and a new beginning.[9]

Forgiveness doesn't mean something didn't happen. It doesn't mean it didn't hurt. It doesn't mean it was ok. Forgiveness means it no longer has the power to control your life.

It is important to understand that forgiveness and trust are not the same thing. Forgiveness is given freely, but trust must be rebuilt. (Especially if there has been abuse or there are other serious issues present.) The wisdom of God would say be careful and use godly discernment in trusting that person again. Forgiving someone doesn't mean you're obligated to keep them in your life. A wise man once said, "Forgiveness is a gift you give yourself." Forgiveness cannot undo the past, but it can keep your past from undoing your future.

Don't let unforgiveness keep you locked out of God's best for your life. Unlock the trapdoor of unforgiveness and throw away the key. Choose to let God be bigger than your hurt and lead you into a future that's bigger than your past. Great things await beyond the barriers of unforgiveness.

Evaluate / Eliminate / Elevate

Evaluate: Is there anyone you're holding bitterness or unforgiveness toward? (Many people have bitterness or unforgiveness toward themselves or even toward God without even realizing it. While God has never sinned or wronged us, many times we hold resentment toward him because we are angry about things that have taken place. God doesn't "need" our forgiveness, but we need the freedom that comes from forgiving and letting go of any anger, bitterness and resentment we have toward him.)

Eliminate: What are the specific things you need to forgive—"to give up completely"—in order to heal and move forward? (Sometimes it can be a helpful exercise to list whom you need to forgive and what you need to forgive them for. Pray through the list, releasing your hurt and that person to God. When you're through, throw away the list.)

Elevate: Have the hurts you've experienced caused you to believe something that doesn't line up with God's Word—about yourself, about God, about others, about your future? What truths from God's Word do you need to hold on to as you work toward healing? ("I am accepted and loved by God, even if I am rejected by people . . ." "I am valuable, even if I make mistakes . . .")

eight

Believe Big, Hustle Hard

Persistence can change failure into
extraordinary achievement.

Matt Biondi

Louie was a troublemaker. He started smoking at age six, got
into fights with students and teachers at school, and chewed
raw garlic to keep the other kids away from him. When he
became an altar boy, he stole the priests' wine.

He and his friends would often roam the streets at night
looking for mischief. After the shops would close, he'd use
a heavy wire with a hook at the end to reach through the
cracks in the windows and snag candy, cigarettes, and baked
goods. His friends eventually began to call him "the Brain"
because he could always figure out how to get away with
their shenanigans.

But the troublemaking caught up to Louie in his early
teenage years. Finally the day came when everyone had

enough. As the police and Louie's parents came to their wits' end, his older brother, Pete, suggested a punishment that, unlike the others, just might work. There was one thing Louie could do well after all his years of getting into trouble: *run.*

Pete, an excellent athlete, stood up for Louie and negotiated a deal that could give him a second chance: if Louie played sports as part of his punishment, his lengthy list of demerits would be cleared. The principal reluctantly agreed to give Louie one last chance to get his act together, and the choice was left in Louie's hands.

In his book *Don't Give Up, Don't Give In*, Olympic athlete and World War II prisoner of war Louie Zamperini describes his years as a delinquent youth and the pivotal moment when he was forced to make a decision that would impact the course of his entire life.

> The prospect of starting ninth grade with a clean slate was irresistible. All I had to do was run. "I guess I will if you force me to," I told Pete. "No one is going to force you to do anything," he said. "You're old enough now to make a decision. You can continue in your rotten life and end up in prison or work in a steel mill or an oil field for peanuts. Or you can run and try to accomplish something."[1]

Louie's first track meet was a disaster. He finished last, exhausted and wheezing from his smoking habit. He wanted to quit, but he knew if he did, his deal with the principal would be off the table. A week later, Louie ran his second race, this time coming in third.

> Afterward I realized I had to make a big decision: be a trouble-maker or a runner? I loved the new recognition from running,

but was it worth it? Yes. I began to train as diligently as I had caused mischief.[2]

Can You See It?

Louie credits much of his success to his brother's influence in his life. Pete worked hard, helping him train and spurring him on. It quickly became evident that Louie had a gift. After his first win, he went undefeated for three and a half years. He continued to break records and ran in the 1936 Olympics in Berlin.[3] Louie's potential had been there all along; the game changer was someone seeing that potential and being willing to take a risk and invest in it.

There's a parable I love in Luke 13. Jesus shares a story of a man who saw the potential of what was before him and decided to do everything in his power to see it convert to reality.

> Then he told this parable: "A man had a fig tree growing in his vineyard, and he went to look for fruit on it but did not find any. So he said to the man who took care of the vineyard, 'For three years now I've been coming to look for fruit on this fig tree and haven't found any. Cut it down! Why should it use up the soil?'
>
> "'Sir,' the man replied, 'leave it alone for one more year, and I'll dig around it and fertilize it. If it bears fruit next year, fine! If not, then cut it down.'" (vv. 6–9)

For some reason, this tree wasn't producing fruit. We don't know why, but the owner was clearly frustrated and ready to give up. Most of us have been there too. The owner's response is exactly how most of us, myself included, react to situations that aren't producing results the way we want. "Cut it down . . . get rid of it. Let's move on."

But I love the vineyard keeper; he speaks up with a completely different approach. Instead of neglecting the struggling tree, he suggests they lean in and do the opposite—put in *more* work and give it *more* care and attention. Why? Because he could see the possibility of what it might produce.

When things go wrong, most of the time our human nature's response is to withdraw our effort rather than to press in, to add more effort, to think of new strategies. We'd usually rather walk away than work a little bit harder.

But what if we took the same approach as this vineyard keeper and applied it to the areas of our life where we're struggling to produce the results we want? Instead of pulling back, giving up, and neglecting them, what if we lean in and give just a little bit more for just a little bit longer? Add in more effort and develop some new strategies that might produce change?

The vineyard keeper in this little parable can teach us a powerful two-part approach for cultivating success and progress in any area of our life: *believe big* and *hustle hard*.

We see it threaded throughout Louie Zamperini's story too. Because his brother was willing to see potential and make an investment, Louie began to see the potential within himself too. Once he began to apply himself, the results were far greater than anyone could have ever imagined. The kid who everyone thought would amount to nothing completely turned his life around and put his town on the map. But it took a lot of believing big and hustling hard for that potential to be unlocked.

1. Believe big.

Sometimes the greatest potential is locked up in the most unlikely places. The town rabble-rouser who appeared to have the least potential turned out to have the most. Louie's brother stepped up and took a risk because he believed there was something more inside of Louie—even though he hadn't seen it yet.

The same was true for the vineyard keeper. In the midst of the discouraging reality of the circumstances, he was still looking forward; still seeing his future through the filter of faith and possibility rather than discouragement and frustration. He had the courage and boldness to believe for something no one else could see.

One of the most important things we need to plant inside us is faith to believe change is possible. It may look impossible. But our sight isn't the gauge for our faith (2 Cor. 5:7). This vineyard keeper had been waiting for three years for this tree to produce fruit . . . and nothing happened. He had no tangible evidence to believe the coming year would be any different, but it didn't stop him from believing.

But notice—he didn't just *believe* the next year would be different, he took some practical steps toward improving the situation! He knew what the odds were, but he was determined to give it his best shot at beating them.

And what was his weapon of choice for beating the odds? *Hustle.*

2. Hustle hard.

If we want change, we have to dare to believe big but then match that belief with an equally strong commitment to hustle hard.

Notice what this guy said: "*I'll dig around it and fertilize it.*" He was willing to dig down a little and break up the hard spots. To bump up against some resistance. To prepare the

139

soil and add some necessary ingredients to improve its health. His vision would require work on his part. But it was a price he was willing to pay—even without the guarantee of success.

Over the years, I've met a lot of people who have a huge vision for their lives and what they want to accomplish for God. But unfortunately, a lot of times their vision outweighs their hustle. They have big dreams and plans, but they're just not willing to put in the work and sacrifice required to make it happen.

It seems like some people are just allergic to hard work. We all know that guy at the office—the one who can always find an excuse whenever something needs to be done. Even if he doesn't have anything to do all day, as soon as you need a hand with something, suddenly a sinus headache strikes or he's swamped and can't help. Some people put more effort into getting out of work than it would take to actually do the work!

Some of us have heard the saying, "You can't have a million-dollar dream with a minimum-wage work ethic." It's true. God does have an incredible, significant plan for our life, but it won't just happen on its own. Our level of hustle has to rise to the level of our vision if we want it to become a reality.

But what exactly is hustle? I like to define it this way: *hustle is a commitment to work hard fueled by a drive to succeed.* When we're hustling, it means we're getting after it, beating the bushes, doing whatever it takes, going the extra mile.

Some people may think hustle and hard work are the same thing, but there's an important distinction. We can work hard without having any hustle. Someone who has hustle is ambitious and self-motivated; they're looking to get things done. Hustle makes us stand out from the crowd and helps us win in life.

Going the Distance

In November 1976, the *New York Times* ran a piece telling a real-life rags-to-riches story about a man who, one year earlier, despite having big dreams for his life, was running out of options. His wife was pregnant, his bull mastiff was starving, and he couldn't pay the rent on their tiny, rundown apartment. He had $106 in his bank account and not a lot of options.

What he *did* have was a story that had been brewing inside of him for a while. He decided the time had come to let it out. In three and a half days, he wrote a movie script he was determined to sell to producers and get himself back on the path to financial stability. He got up every morning at 6:00 a.m. and wrote it out by hand with a Bic pen, then handed the pages to his wife, who typed them up. And when it was done, he went knocking on doors.

It worked. Producers liked the script, but there was one catch. He refused to sell the script without an agreement that he could also star in the leading role, and producers weren't interested. He was a struggling actor with little experience. But with his wife's unwavering support, he held out, turning down offers upward of $200,000.

He eventually succeeded in selling the movie to producers who were willing to take a chance and agreed to let him play the lead. That man was Sylvester Stallone and that movie was *Rocky*. The movie that almost didn't get made with the actor nobody wanted went on to win the Oscar for Best Picture in 1977.[4]

"Believe big, hustle hard" should be a way of life for us. When things are good, believe big and hustle hard. When things are bad, believe bigger and hustle harder. There may be a lot of things we can't do, but we can always make the choice to believe big and hustle hard. It just might be the key that changes everything.

How to Get Your Hustle On

People who hustle are more likely to win in life. That's just how it works. Sure, sometimes people with less-than-impressive work ethics get a lucky break, but most people who experience sustained success have made hustle a habit. Whether it's our health, finances, relationships, parenting, or any other area, a commitment to work hard fueled by a desire to succeed is going to be essential to moving forward.

Hustle Habit #1: Be diligent.

Diligence is a principle found all over the Bible, and it's one of the keys for a successful life. Diligence can be defined as "giving the degree of care required in a given situation; a persevering determination to perform a task;"[5] or "the opposite of negligence."[6]

I like to think of diligence as focused tenacity. Diligence sees the target, persistently puts out the effort to get there, and doesn't give up until that target is in hand. Like my pastor, Don Matheny, says, "It's like a bulldog on a mailman." Diligence is staying late to finish a project you committed to get done. It's going the extra mile to get it right. It's pressing on, even when it's tough.

Most of us have been on the other side of someone else's lack of diligence, or negligence. A sloppy job on a project at work, poorly prepared food and apathetic service at a restaurant, or a friend who didn't keep his or her word. We don't enjoy the effects of other people's negligence. But sadly enough, our own negligence can be one of the biggest reasons our life doesn't look the way we want it to. We can't have healthy, thriving relationships if we're too busy or self-focused to invest in them. We can't expect our physical bodies to stay well and strong if we don't care for them the way we know we should. Even things like our material possessions or our finances can suffer if neglect creeps into our daily habits. Anyone who's ever gotten hit with a fine or a late fee knows how much neglect can cost!

When we're negligent on managing the practical areas of our life, we can end up constantly late, unable to find things, stressed out, or behind on life in general.

When my daughter Anna was in fifth grade, we had to make a photo timeline of her life. We hadn't done a great job of organizing pictures, so when her assignment hit we kind of had a little moment of panic. We had one huge box of pictures, with no order to them, and we had to sort through them all one by one to try to find all the different pictures she needed. While it wasn't major in the grand scheme of life, having our photos organized sure would have been easier and less stressful for a small fifth-grade project! If we make a habit of being negligent in the little things, it can add up to a lot of frustration, anxiety, and wasted time in our life.

Negligence always ends up costing us. It's easy to see how close the word *negligence* is to the word *negate*. *Negate* means "to cause to be ineffective or invalid."[7] I wonder how many times we have negated God's promises in our life by simply not diligently caring for something the way we should?

Ouch! I know this might sting a little. But the heart behind this is in no way to condemn or discourage anyone. What I've found in serving and leading people is that so often people want to succeed, but negligence keeps stealing their momentum. Whether intentionally or accidentally, they are neglecting the blessings and opportunities God has put in their hand and around them. That blocks their ability to move forward. What we care for grows and thrives; what we neglect suffers and dies.

This isn't just limited to the practical areas of our life. Diligence and negligence can directly affect our ability to thrive spiritually and flourish in the call God has placed on our life. Romans 11:29 tells us, "God's gifts and his call can never be withdrawn" (NLT). The gift and calling on our life will never change, but how we choose to walk them out and steward them is up to us.

Second Chronicles 29:11 says, "My sons, do not be negligent *and* careless now, for the LORD has chosen you to stand in His presence, to attend to His service, and to be His ministers" (AMP). What an incredible thought to know we have been chosen by God to serve him and to be used for his purposes! But we also see that with the call a word of caution is given. The author is saying, "Because God has chosen you, make sure you aren't negligent or careless!" He knew negligence is one of the greatest enemies to the calling and purpose we've been chosen for.

Diligence is more than just what we do; it's a spirit that defines our life. It's a quality we build into the fabric of our character. When we do, it brings rewards into our life. The Bible is full of verses about diligence and the benefits it brings, but let's focus on these three:

1. **Wealth.** "Lazy hands make for poverty, but diligent hands bring wealth" (Prov. 10:4).

2. **Satisfaction.** "A sluggard's appetite is never filled, but the desires of the diligent are fully satisfied" (Prov. 13:4).

3. **Promotion.** "Work hard and become a leader; be lazy and become a slave" (Prov. 12:24 NLT).

Diligence positions us to unlock all the potential that God has put *in* us and *around* us.

I'm so thankful for the people in my world, and over the years I've had the opportunity to be around some very successful individuals. As I've gotten to know them, I've noticed some characteristics they all have in common:

1. They don't give up easily.
2. They go the extra mile.
3. They're finishers.
4. They know details make the difference.

Diligence may not always seem like an exciting or life-changing quality, but I promise you—it matters. As Steve Jobs, cofounder of Apple Inc., often said, "Details matter. It's worth waiting to get it right."[8]

Hustle Habit #2: Work IN it and ON it.

It's not enough to just work *hard*; we've got to work *smart*. I think of hustle like a coin with two sides—heads and tails. The "tails" side is hard work. This is where we get down and work *in* it. We get our rear in gear, get down to the nitty-gritty, and work our tail off. There is just no substitute for hard work. You've probably heard the saying, "Anything in life worth having is worth working for." And it's true! We can't expect things to just fall in our lap. If we want something, we need to be willing to work for it.

But that's only one part of the equation. From time to time, we need to pull up out of the actual work we're doing and think about *what* we are doing. This is the "heads" side of the coin—we're using our mind to work *on* it. We ask ourselves, *Is what I'm doing working? Am I getting the right results? What changes could I make to be more effective?*

If we only work "in it," we can end up with the treadmill effect: working hard all the time but not getting anywhere. You've probably heard the saying that insanity is doing the same thing over and over and expecting different results. In order to keep making progress, we have to make sure we're working hard *on the right things*! Lee Cockerell, former executive vice president of operations for the Walt Disney World Resort, said, "'Efficient' is being able to get things done. 'Effective' is doing the right things in the right order, and making sure you address everything that is urgent, vital and important, in every part of your life."[9]

Hustle Habit #3: Stay passionate.

In 2 Timothy 1:6, Paul tells Timothy, "Stir up the gift of God which is in you" (NKJV). What's inside you does not automatically produce results; it needs to be drawn out and cultivated.

Louie Zamperini's brother Pete spoke to the gift and the potential he recognized, but ultimately Louie had to make the choice to believe he could change and succeed. He had to hustle hard to train and develop his gift. No one else could use his gift for him. The same is true with you. No one else can fulfill your potential but you.

The people in your life can inspire you, challenge you, and help you develop, but at the end of the day, the decision is up to you: will you believe big and hustle hard? Will you do what it takes to see the possibilities God placed within you drawn out and let them be worked, challenged, strengthened, and refined? Will you give them the chance to have life breathed into them and go from possibility to reality? Only you can decide.

Hustle Habit #4: Stick it out when things get tough.

When I was fifteen, I got my first checking account. I was so excited to have a checkbook of my very own. It was like a badge of freedom. After we got everything set up at the bank, my mom tried to give me some directions on how to balance a checkbook—writing down all the entries, accounting for any fees, keeping track of my balance—all that good stuff. Stuff I should have listened to. (Especially since she was a CPA and really knew what she was talking about!)

But I thought I knew everything and had places to be and things to do. Who has time to be bothered with something like how to balance a checkbook?

As it turns out, I *did* have time to be bothered with it, because a few months later my independence came to a screeching halt. I had bounced numerous checks (to put it mildly) and my account was frozen. I'm not even going to mention how overdrawn I was. Let's just say I had gotten myself into a gigantic mess.

I remember thinking, *Man, I'm so confused. I still have checks left. What's the problem?* I can't help but laugh at my seriously flawed strategy for financial management.

I went to my mom and I told her, "Mom, I messed everything up big-time. Can you help me?" My sweet and gracious mom sat down with me and, once again, helped me learn how to handle a checking account. And you better believe that this time I listened.

As we were working through the mess of my checkbook, I told her, "I'm not going to bank there anymore. I'm going to close this account and start over at another bank. It's way too embarrassing for me. Those ladies will laugh every time they see me."

Though my mom was sweet and gracious, she was also wise and firm. She said, "Nope. That's not how we do things. You're going to get things in order and learn how to do this. If you want to switch to another bank in a couple of months, that's fine, but we're going to get this worked out first."

I'm so grateful my mom had the strength and wisdom to make me see that situation through. It wasn't an easy lesson to learn, but it's one that has stuck with me through the rest of my life. What I learned was when things get tough, you don't just quit or find a way out. You have the character, integrity, and discipline to keep going and stick it out to the end. As poet Robert Frost wrote, the best way out is always through.[10]

Choose to be faithful to what you started. Faithfulness has rewards, so keep working even when it's hard. Even when the fun and excitement of a new opportunity has turned into the mundane routine of a daily grind. Even when you're in the middle of a problem that's frustrating and confusing. Even when your circumstances are painful and unfair. People with hustle keep pressing through until they've achieved their goal.

At the 1938 NCAA championships, Louie Zamperini ran one of the most challenging races of his career. Other runners intentionally tried to take him out, boxing him in, cursing at him, even hurting him physically. One runner punctured Louie's little toe with his spikes, another gashed his shins, and another elbowed him with such force it cracked a rib. But Louie refused to be deterred and not only finished the race but set the national collegiate record. It stood for the next fifteen years. He didn't know it at the time, but the same qualities of perseverance and persistence that helped him succeed as a runner would later help him survive as a soldier in World War II.[11]

Hebrews 10:36–39 encourages us to stay the course no matter what:

> But you need to stick it out, staying with God's plan so you'll be there for the promised completion.
>> It won't be long now, he's on the way;
>>> he'll show up most any minute.
>> But anyone who is right with me thrives on loyal trust;
>>> if he cuts and runs, I won't be very happy.
> But we're not quitters who lose out. Oh, no! We'll stay with it and survive, trusting all the way. (MSG)

Hard work is part of the key to unlocking God's plan for our life. It simply can't unfold without it. The things we desire—the vision we have for our life—won't just happen. God didn't design it to work that way. He intends for us to be an active part of the process. Faith and diligence don't always come naturally, but they are two things that pay off, in both the spiritual and the natural world. As author and business expert Jim Collins says, "The real path to greatness, it turns out, requires simplicity and diligence."[12]

Believe big. Hustle hard. Do your best—and trust God to do the rest.

Evaluate / Eliminate / Elevate

Evaluate: Are there areas of your life that are not thriving or producing fruit the way you wish they were? Where do you need to believe bigger or hustle harder?

Eliminate: Sometimes we are neglecting important areas of our life without fully realizing it. Are there any areas you need to devote more time and attention to in order to see them thrive (long-term and short-term)?

Elevate: List one specific step you can take for each area where you'd like to see change take place.

nine

The Seven Pillars of Financial Wisdom

What you do with money shows you
who you really are.

Dave Ramsey

Have you ever wished somebody would write you a check for a million dollars? Sounds like a dream come true, right? Maybe . . . but not necessarily. *Time* magazine recently published an article called, "Here's How Winning The Lottery Makes You Miserable." It highlighted five people who won and what they had to say about winning. As surprising as it might sound, I couldn't help but feel sorry for most of them.

When Jack Whittaker won $315 million in 2002, he was already a millionaire. Four years later his money was gone and he was grieving many personal losses, including a daughter and a granddaughter who had died from drug overdoses. In one interview he said, "I wish that we had torn the ticket up . . . I just don't like Jack Whittaker. I don't like the hard heart I've got. I don't like what I've become."

After winning $30 million, Abraham Shakespeare told his brother all the time, "I'd have been better off broke." In 2007, Donna Mikkin won $34.5 million. On her blog, she wrote, "If you asked me, my life was hijacked by the lottery." Winning the lottery didn't take away all her worries or solve all her problems. In fact, she says it led to "emotional bankruptcy." She went on to say, "Most of us think that winning the lottery is the ultimate fulfillment. But I found that wasn't the case."

Richard Lustig is one of the few to defy the odds by hanging on to most of his winnings and his happiness. He said the key was hiring a good financial planner and a good accountant after he paid off all his debts. He said it's easy to "think there's no tomorrow. Well, there is a tomorrow and eventually [the money] will run out."[1]

There's no way around it: finances are a big deal. So many people struggle beneath the burden of money-related challenges and issues. Money's role and impact in our life is so much bigger than just our finances. Matthew 6:21 tells us that where our treasure is, our heart is too. When we think about this in the context of Proverbs 4:23, which teaches that everything we do flows from our heart, we see that there is a very clear, powerful connection between our heart and our "treasure." If not handled properly, money has the potential to bring destruction into our life on multiple levels.

Getting Your House in Order

On average, Americans spend $1.33 for every dollar earned.[2] Gloria Arenson, author of *Born to Spend* and a marriage and family therapist, says, "We are more and more stressed out as a society and for some people, an outlet to this stress is buying stuff."[3] People are increasingly using spending as a coping mechanism.

Here are some sobering statistics:

- The average household is paying a total of $6,658 in interest per year, with $2,630 of that amount being interest on credit card debt. That comes to 9 percent of the average household income being spent on *interest* alone![4]

- A recent survey found 1 in 4 people's number one thought daily is money. The same survey revealed the top three financial concerns people have are living paycheck to paycheck, living in debt forever, and never being able to retire.[5]

- In an annual survey by the American Psychological Association, money is consistently ranked as Americans' number one source of stress.[6]

- Nearly 75 percent of all adults feel stressed about money at least some of the time.[7]

Financial pressure is actually so much bigger than just a money issue because it can bring devastation to so many different parts of our life. As if the direct effects of financial problems weren't enough—not being able to pay your bills, buy food, or provide basic necessities—the secondary effects of financial pressure have been linked to stress-induced physical and mental health problems and damaged relationships, just to name a few. The stress of financial pressure can cause breakdown in every area of our life.

Here's the good news: there's a better way—God's way. Isaiah 55:8–9 tells us our ways aren't like God's and reminds us his ways are better. Even if our financial lives are a wreck and the weight of financial strain is taking its toll on us, God's Word can give us the tools we need to put it all back together.

The Bible has over eight hundred verses giving advice on the topic of money and money management.[8] The Bible calls it wisdom. *Wisdom* is a word we're all familiar with, but what does it really mean? I like to define it this way: *wisdom is knowledge and truth practically applied.*

Contrary to what most people think, more money isn't the solution to money problems. In fact, most people's "money problems" aren't really money problems at all; they're management problems. In his book *Rich Dad, Poor Dad*, Robert Kiyosaki puts it this way: "Intelligence solves problems and produces money. Money without financial intelligence is money soon gone."[9] It doesn't matter how much money you have if you keep making unwise choices.

The principle of "God's part/my part" we've talked about is especially significant in the financial area of our life. Seeking out wisdom is "my part" in the equation for healthy finances. All over the book of Proverbs we see specific principles God gives us to help us manage our money his way.

Proverbs 9:1 personifies wisdom as a woman who has "built her house; she has set up its seven pillars." From this we gather that wisdom serves to establish and expand our life while also bringing a sense of strength and stability.

In the Bible, seven is the number of perfection or completion. Wisdom fills in the gaps in our life; it makes sure that we are covered and "completed" so that no areas are left vulnerable. Let's pull out seven pillars of financial wisdom from Proverbs that will help us build a strong financial "house."

First Things First

Our priorities are reflected by our investments. The things we love most will ultimately be reflected in what we give our best to. Proverbs 3:9–10 says, "Honor the LORD with your wealth, with the firstfruits of all your crops; then your barns will be filled to overflowing, and your vats will brim over with new wine."

Pillar #1: Honor.

Honor is the first pillar because it's the most important. Everything else in our life should flow from a place of honor for God. The Bible says, "Every good and perfect gift is from God" (James 1:17 NIrV). We may have some financial limitations, but we need to make the choice to see what we *do* have as a gift from God. The question is, *Are you honoring God with the things he's blessed you with?*

Honor means "to show respect; to revere." It literally means "to worship." So when the Bible says, "Honor the LORD with your wealth, with the firstfruits," it is talking about the principle of tithing. In the Old Testament, when the first crops started to appear, they took them to the temple. It was a way to thank God for the harvest he'd brought and express trust in him for what was to come.

155

I love to teach on tithing because it's so incredibly powerful, and yet I find it's one of the subjects people are the most confused about. I could fill a book with the stories of people in our church whose lives have been changed simply by starting to obey this one principle.

The word *tithe* by definition means "tenth" or "ten percent."[10] The concept of tithing isn't something the modern church or a group of pastors came up with. Tithing was God's idea and it spans every era of God's relationship with his people. We see it all the way back in Genesis 14, when Abraham, who was still called "Abram" at that point, brought a tithe to God and gave it to the priest Melchizedek. It continues to be threaded through the Word of God, into the New Testament, where Jesus told us we should tithe in Matthew 23:23. It is part of God's plan for a healthy life.

To get a better understanding of this powerful principle, we can look to Malachi 3:8–10, one of the most extensive passages in the Bible about tithing:

> "Will a mere mortal rob God? Yet you rob me.
>
> "But you ask, 'How are we robbing you?'
>
> "In tithes and offerings. You are under a curse—your whole nation—because you are robbing me. Bring the whole tithe into the storehouse, that there may be food in my house. Test me in this," says the LORD Almighty, "and see if I will not throw open the floodgates of heaven and pour out so much blessing that there will not be room enough to store it."

Let me give you a simple definition for tithing based on this passage: *tithing is giving the first 10 percent of our income to God through our local church*. In this passage, it's clear God's people were having some money trouble.

As we read, we see a problem, a process, a purpose, and a promise.

- **The problem:** you're under a curse. Picture a little hamster running in his wheel . . . working so hard, but getting nowhere. The faster he runs, the faster he . . . goes nowhere. Maybe you can relate. You're working, striving, and struggling, and it's still tough to make ends meet. It feels like no matter what you do, you can't get ahead. There's no financial momentum or peace.

- **The process:** bring the *whole* tithe into the storehouse. In the Bible, "storehouse" is used interchangeably for "church," "temple," or "house of God." You bring 10 percent of your income to your church. You may think you can't afford to tithe, but the truth is you can't afford *not* to tithe. The price of disobedience is always more than the cost of obedience.

- **The purpose:** that there may be food in God's house. This deals with the strength of your church. Not only does the tithe move your life forward as you sow out of faith and obedience but it also moves the work of the church forward. We don't tithe to a charity organization or a missionary friend—we tithe to our local church, where we are planted.

- **The promise:** test God and he will throw open the windows of heaven and bless your life. If we do tithing God's way, then we're positioning ourselves to live under an open heaven and receive God's blessing.

Make tithing your top financial priority each month. Find a way to make it work and adjust the rest of your budget to fit around it. Yes, that means you might have to cut cable and Starbucks, but let me tell you: God's blessing is worth it!

When it comes down to it, tithing is not a money issue—it's a trust issue. Here's the question: *Who are you trusting for your provision?* Are you trusting yourself? Your spouse? Your employer? The government? This economy? Whatever you place your trust in ultimately has first place in your life.

Tithing is all about keeping God first in our life and giving back what already belongs to him. God doesn't "need" our money. But he knows we need the things that tithing accomplishes in our life in order to truly thrive.

If you're a tither—keep tithing! If tithing is new to you, or if you haven't been consistent in it, I encourage you to start tithing regularly to your local church. The key here is *consistently*. Tithing is a principle that must be faithfully, persistently put into action. I'm confident as you do, you'll begin to see God be true to his promise.

Put Some Muscle into It

One of the things I love about the book of Proverbs is all the characters you read about. We see the Fool, the Simpleton, and then there is the Sluggard—the guy who just doesn't want to work. Proverbs 20:4 says, "Sluggards do not plow in season; so at harvest time they look but find nothing." If we put it in today's terms we might say, "Sluggards don't work hard all month; so on payday they look for a check, but find nothing."

Pillar #2: Hard work.

There is a direct correlation between hard work and financial strength, or "wealth" as the Bible often calls it. If you want to have something in life, most of the time it's going to come through hard work.

This verse talks about *plowing*, an agricultural term meaning "to break up and turn up the earth; to move or progress with driving force."[11] In life, just like in agriculture, there are seasons where we plow and seasons where we harvest. When you get a job as a young man or woman, usually after high school or college, it's the start of your plowing season. And for most people it lasts for a long time—usually forty years or more.

In other words, we'd better get used to working! Theodore Roosevelt said, "Far and away the best prize life offers is the chance to work hard at work worth doing."[12] Get ready to put your shoulder into it, because we need to work hard—and then get up and do it again tomorrow. But just as important, we need to "work willingly" at whatever we do, as Colossians 3:23 tells us, "always working for the Lord rather than for people" (NLT).

A "minimum mentality" says, *I'm just going to do the minimum required to get by*. If you have that disposition, then that's the level that you will always operate from—and receive from. You will give the minimum. Your bank account will show the minimum. Your progress will be the minimum. Your return in life will be the minimum.

But if you act from a spirit that says, *I'm going to go above and beyond and do more than what is required of me*, then you'll naturally receive more back.

I once heard it said, "Dreams don't work unless you do." That's pretty accurate. Any dream, any ambition, any goal will come with a price. But if you're willing to pay the price and keep plowing, it will pay off.

Seeing Our Future in 20/20

Jonathan Swift, author of *Gulliver's Travels*, was born into a poor family in the middle of the seventeenth century—a time of great change in Europe politically, socially, and scientifically. Despite his less than advantageous start, Swift's sharp mind and brilliant wit made him an influential political and religious voice in his day. Perhaps he was thinking of his own journey from a poor, fatherless, mediocre student to prominent author and dean of St. Patrick's Cathedral (Dublin) when he said, "Vision is the art of seeing things invisible."[13] If we want to create forward motion in our life, sometimes we have to be able to look beyond how things *are* and see how they *could be*.

Pillar #3: Vision.

Having a vision for our life is one of the most important prerequisites for success. When we have a picture of where we want to be, it's easier to pay the price required to get there. Vision gives us the ability to say no to good things so that we can say yes to great things.

Vision compels us to move forward and keeps us on track. People who lack vision "stumble all over themselves; But when they attend to what [God] reveals, they are most blessed" (Prov. 29:18 MSG). If we feel like we're floundering in life, it's time to check our vision.

It's not only ok to have a vision for healthy finances, it's part of being a good steward. Here are some great things to have a vision for in our finances:

- To be able to tithe, pay our bills, and meet all financial obligations on time.
- To be able to save each month.

- To be able to create an emergency fund.
- To get out of debt.
- To be able to be generous.
- To have the finances to carry out the dreams in our heart.

There's an old Japanese proverb that says, "Vision without action is a daydream. Action without vision is a nightmare." This is especially true in the area of our finances. We need to get a vision for where we want to be and then put our vision into action.

Setting Ourselves Up for Success

Vision and hard work are designed to work together to bring about the promises of God in our life, but there's another element to the equation: good planning. Proverbs 21:5 puts it this way: "Good planning and hard work lead to prosperity, but hasty shortcuts lead to poverty" (NLT).

Pillar #4: Good planning.

If vision is the picture of where we want to go, plans are the bridge we use to get there. Hard work is the effort it takes to walk the bridge. These three work together to develop possibilities into reality.

Have you ever worked really hard on something only to get to the end and realize that, in your haste, you failed to factor a few "minor details" into your plan? After all the hard work, your effort was for nothing. Even if we're willing to work hard, our effort can be short-circuited by lack of planning.

Proverbs 16:3 tells us to commit to the Lord whatever we do, and he will establish our plans. Here's the thing: God can't establish our plans if we haven't made any! A God-honoring plan that's committed to the Lord gives him something to bless.

Some of us are natural planners. Others, not so much. If good planning isn't currently a part of your financial strategy, here are a few very simple, very practical steps to help get you started.

1. **Track your spending for ninety days.** Keep a log of every single dollar you spend. You can do it with good old-fashioned pencil and paper, or download an app for your phone or computer. You might be surprised where your money is going. The good news is, when you know, you can change it.

2. **Create a budget and stick to it.** A budget is simply having a plan for your money—telling your money where you want it to go.

3. **Start saving for your future.** Don't live your life only thinking about your immediate needs and wants. Wisdom tells us to think about what's coming and plan accordingly so that we can be prepared.

Sometimes we shy away from things like planning and budgeting because, if we're honest, we're afraid to know exactly where things are. Bite the bullet and get the cold, hard facts. The things we fail to deal with usually only get worse. Getting an accurate picture is the first step to changing your financial situation.

As the stats at the beginning of the chapter show, finances bring anxiety to so many people. Getting a plan won't necessarily change your situation instantly, but sometimes simply having it all on paper and knowing you have a plan brings a measure of peace right away.

The D-Word

Let's be honest: nobody likes to hear the word *discipline*. But for some of us, lack of discipline is the one thing that is hijacking our financial success. Discipline is often what separates those who become successful from those who don't.

Pillar #5: Discipline.

In their bestselling book, *The Millionaire Next Door*, Thomas J. Stanley, PhD, and William D. Danko, PhD, share this powerful finding: "After twenty years of studying millionaires across a wide spectrum of industries, we have concluded that *the character of the business owner is more important in predicting his level of wealth than the classification of his business.*"[14] Who you are inside impacts your financial life more than anything else.

Self-discipline is one of the most powerful tools you have at your disposal. In 1757, George Washington wrote instructions to his company captains, emphasizing the vital role discipline played in their endeavors: "Discipline is the soul of an army. It makes small numbers formidable; procures success to the weak, and esteem to all."[15] The same is true in our life. Discipline produces transformation. It helps make our weak places strong, improves our odds of success, and gives us a healthy sense of satisfaction. Without question, discipline is an essential ingredient to success.

The truth is, personal finance is much more *personal* than *financial*. The biggest key to managing our finances is usually managing ourselves. A lot of times we want the solution to financial challenges to be something big dropped in our lap—a promotion, a new job, a year-end bonus, a rich uncle found on Ancestry.com. We're waiting for the windfall, but God is directing us toward discipline. When the temptation strikes to begrudge the daily grind of budgeting, working, and staying disciplined in our spending habits, remember "dishonest money dwindles away, but *whoever gathers money little by little makes it grow*" (Prov. 13:11, emphasis added).

What I've found is this is usually how God works in our life—little by little. God may want to give you a new job or a promotion and change things all at once. But he also might want to give you something far more powerful: the discipline to change your life. Sometimes God wants to change our situation—but sometimes he wants to change us.

Most people are only one financial crisis away from financial ruin. Even if you think you don't have anything to save, start somewhere. Open a savings account and put something in every time you get paid, even if it's five or ten dollars to start. Gradually work your way up until you can save 5 to 10 percent of your income each month. The 80/10/10 principle is a great guide to a basic budget: 10 percent is your tithe, 10 percent goes in savings, and you learn to live off of 80 percent.

Discipline is something that pays high dividends in every area of our life, whether it's our health, finances, skill development, relationships, or job. Anywhere we want to have success, we'll need discipline.

The Blessing of the Open Hand

Financial expert Dave Ramsey says, "Outrageous generosity is a character quality of people who win with money."[16] And it's true. A generous spirit is one of the most powerful things we can possess when it comes to being blessed. Generosity is about living an openhanded life. Instead of approaching life with a "closed fist," anxiously clutching everything that's ours, we take an openhanded approach, finding joy in the opportunity to share, give, and pour out blessing to others.

Pillar #6: Generosity.

Consider the gospel from God's point of view. John 3:16 tells us, "God so loved the world that he *gave*" (emphasis added). The story of the cross carries an abundantly clear message: *generosity is the essence of godliness*. If you are going to say, "I want to be more like God," then you're going to have to be a generous person! God has been so gracious and generous with us, it's only right that we as Christians should be the most vibrant examples of generosity the world has ever seen.

This is about so much more than just our finances. Generosity should be the overarching spirit characterizing every part of our life. When we have a generous spirit, generosity flows from the core of our being and shows up in everything we do. This means we should be:

- **Generous in our thoughts.** Choose to believe the best about people, thinking positive thoughts and having positive opinions toward them. Don't be small-minded, critical, or cynical. Love people with no strings attached.

None of us are perfect, so give people lots of grace and the freedom to be themselves.

- **Generous in our words.** Go the extra mile to build people up with life-giving words. Give a compliment. Tell them you appreciate them. Find a genuine reason to say something nice to someone.

- **Generous in our time.** Don't fill your life so full you can't give anyone your time. Build a measure of margin into your life so that you can be generous with your time. We can't be a blessing if we are always running on a deficit.

- **Generous in our finances.** The world might tell us generosity doesn't make sense financially—that the more you give, the less you have. But God's kingdom operates in a completely differently way; generosity actually *paves the way* for blessing to come into our life!

In Proverbs 11:17 we see a powerful illustration of the impact a generous spirit has on our life: "The merciful, kind and generous man benefits himself [for his deeds return to bless him]" (AMP-CE). Generosity is like a boomerang. The things we release come back to bless us. We don't give to get something back; that's just a natural by-product. We give because it's what the Bible tells us to do and because it's what God has done for us. Jesus said, "Freely you have received; freely give" (Matt. 10:8). There's no better way to model God's love than living generously with wide-open hearts and hands.

Graced for a Place

One summer I was visiting Newport Beach, and some of our friends took us to this amazing place called The Wedge. As the waves hit the rocks, the impact doubles their height and power and gives them a distinctive wedge shape. Every now and then the waves are massive. It's incredible to see, but it can be really dangerous too. Thousands of people have been sent to the hospital for different kinds of injuries; some have been paralyzed or even killed.

That day I saw a group of guys surfing, trying to catch a big wave. I noticed one surfer who had lost his way a little bit. He was struggling and started moving closer to the rocks. All of a sudden, two lifeguards grabbed their gear and just went tearing into the water with these huge tubes. When they reached him, they pulled him out beyond the dangerous waves. Pretty soon a big lifeguard boat zoomed in and picked him up. I said to my friend Jonathan, "Well, that's kind of embarrassing." He replied, "Yeah, it *is* kind of embarrassing, but better to be embarrassed and live to surf another day!"

What a great thought that applies to any area of our life! We can either be a little embarrassed about being rescued or we can be too proud to ask for help and risk losing it all. Some of us are very good at putting on a front and acting like everything is great—when in reality the ship is sinking. Unfortunately, one of the areas we do this the most with is our finances.

Pillar #7: Humility.

Humility might not be something you would think of as a pillar to financial success, but it is! Proverbs 22:4 shows us an interesting connection to money: "Humility is the fear of the LORD; its wages are riches and honor and life." A humble spirit enables us to ask for help when we are in over our head. We may feel a little embarrassed in the moment, but the dividends that it pays later will be huge.

Humility is so powerful because pride creates spiritual resistance but humility brings divine empowerment. James 4:6 tells us God resists the proud *but gives grace to the humble*. That grace is the empowerment God gives us for the season at hand. It carries a "catch," if you will, though—it's only good for the place God has called you to right here, right now. Proverbs 28:19–20 tells us, "Those who work their land will have abundant food, but those who chase fantasies will have their fill of poverty. A faithful person will be richly blessed, but one eager to get rich will not go unpunished."

These verses tell us to guard against reaching beyond the limits of what God has given us right here and right now. We are graced for a place. God's grace doesn't sustain and empower us when we try to go live life in someone else's place. Work *your* land, stay faithful in *your* place. There is abundance when you're planted in the place you've been graced for.

I encourage you to let God's principles be your ultimate standard and guide for your financial priorities and decisions—above your wants, your plans, your current habits or old mindsets about money. Dave Ramsey says, "When you base your life on principle, 99 percent of your decisions are already made."[17] Let the wisdom of God's Word guide you forward, and build a life that's healthy and honoring to him.

Evaluate / Eliminate / Elevate

Evaluate: Are the seven pillars of financial wisdom present in your life (honor, hard work, vision, good planning, discipline, generosity, and humility)? Which ones aren't as strong as they should be?

Eliminate: Is there a financial habit or mindset that is sabotaging your financial health?

Elevate: List out any new financial habits or mindsets you need to cultivate. What is one practical step you can take to implement it right away?

For more details, a monthly budget guide, and recommended resources, see the appendix.

ten

Don't Hate
While You Wait

Patience is bitter but its fruit is sweet.

Jean Chardin

Nothing I have ever done has been more frustrating than learning to play golf. *Nothing.* Planting a church has been hard at times—but amazing. Parenting has been hard at times—but rewarding. Learning to play golf is frustrating—*all the time*. It's been this on-again, off-again nemesis in my life. Golf and I have a love/hate relationship. I'm hoping one day it'll be a lot more love and a lot less hate.

I wish someone could give me a pill that I could take every night for thirty days and it'd make me a great golfer. The reality is that I don't want to *learn* how to play golf. I want to *play* golf. And I want to do it well. What I *need* to do is take more lessons and master the basic skills and techniques.

But what I'd *like* to do is just get out there and play. I always have this underlying expectation that one day I'll just show up and start playing better. Unfortunately, it hasn't happened yet.

I can get frustrated with the learning process and "check out," which leaves me exactly at the same skill level. Or I can be patient enough to go through the learning process and get everything I can out of it, knowing the frustrating learning phase is a determining factor in the overall success of my golf game.

Learning how to play golf, like many other things in life, doesn't happen overnight. It takes time and patience. And therein lies the root of my problem. American sportswriter Grantland Rice summed it up perfectly when he said, "Golf gives you an insight into human nature."[1] I'm just not a patient person by nature!

I've come a long way in overcoming some of my impatient tendencies, but it's an area I have to continually work on and let God develop in me. It seems I'm not alone in my not-so-patient personality. Engineers at Google say 40 percent of users move on to a different website if it takes more than three seconds to load. Even a quarter of a second delay influences internet users to switch to a competing website.[2]

This is more than just a stat about our internet usage habits; it's a reflection of the culture we live in and the attitude our society has adopted. We want to have exactly what we want and we want to have it now—no denial, no delays. But you've probably heard the phrase, "Good things come to those who wait." Turns out it's true. And it's biblical. The writer of Hebrews tells us not to become lazy, but instead "to be like those who believe and are patient, and so receive what God has promised" (6:12 GNT). Yes, patience is hard work, but the promise is worth it.

Hustle, but Don't Hurry

As ironic as it sounds, progress often comes by being patient. Remember the guy in Luke 13 who believed big and hustled hard? He had the courage and audacity to believe that there could be some fruit from that tree and then worked hard to see it come to pass. But there's another factor in the equation that's worth noting: his patience. If you remember, he had already waited three years to see some fruit. Now he was willing to wait another. He was willing to wait four years for the *possibility* of producing fruit. Some of us have trouble waiting four *days*.

To receive what God has promised, we need to believe big and hustle hard—but we also need to wait well. Patience is part of God's equation for receiving his promises. There is a certain finesse we need to have as we navigate our journey forward. In the midst of the vision, hard work, and passion that faith produces, we have to simultaneously develop the strength of character to be patient and trust in God's timing. We can't let our hustle turn into hurry.

Here's a great definition of patience:

> Patience is the state of endurance under difficult circumstances . . . persevering in the face of delay or provocation without acting on annoyance/anger in a negative way; exhibiting forbearance when under strain, especially when faced with longer-term difficulties. Patience is the level of endurance one's character can take before negativity.[3]

Sometimes we think patience and waiting are the same, but there's a significant difference. Patience works hard at maintaining the right character and a great attitude in the face of delay. Waiting, on the other hand, simply endures the passing of time—often while tapping a foot, crossing arms, rolling eyes, and checking the watch every thirty seconds, asking, "Am I done yet?" (followed by an exasperated sigh). We can't be mad, frustrated, discouraged, *and* patient at the same time!

Maybe you've heard the term *hater* thrown around. It's talking about someone who's bitter, frustrated, negative, and critical. That's the exact opposite of what the Bible says to do to receive God's promises. Even though it's tough, don't hate while you wait!

Keep the Faith

We heard the dictionary definition of patience, now here's the biblical definition: *waiting on God with a positive attitude and a spirit of faith.*

When things don't go exactly according to our timeline, it's easy to let negativity set in or get restless and try to work things out on our own timeline. I know this, because I've done it!

Throughout high school and into college, Leslie and I kind of had an on-again, off-again dating history. Both of us were still growing in our relationship with God and learning how to navigate life as young adults. During that time, I went through a season where I was really trying to get some clarity about God's plan for my life and my future.

I told Leslie that I felt like I needed to take some time to step back and have a season apart to really seek God. And I did—for about a day. After that, it got really tough. I think I stuck with my plan for about three more days before I caved in and wrote Leslie the longest letter I'd ever written.

I poured out my heart on page after page, telling her how much I loved her, how I knew she was the one, and on and on. I sealed it up, put it in the mailbox, and anxiously waited to hear back. Day after day, I'd check the mail for her reply. And day after day, nothing.

Finally the day came when an envelope arrived addressed in her perfect handwriting. Much to my dismay, inside the envelope was *my* letter to her, unopened, with the words "Return to Sender" written across the front.

I couldn't believe it! But after the shock wore off, I admired Leslie's steadfast commitment to let that season have its place and do its work. Her steadfastness is one of her greatest qualities and one of the things I value and love most about her.

In the end, my impatience didn't have any major long-term effects. Down the road, we got married, and twenty-five years later our relationship is healthy and thriving. But trying to work things out in my own wisdom and timing, instead of trusting God's timing, did complicate the situation. And in all honesty, sometimes our impatience can have serious, lasting consequences.

You've probably heard it said, "The right thing at the wrong time is still the wrong thing." God's best in our timing ceases to truly be *his* best. It has now become *our* best, which can never compare.

Most of us would say we want God's best for our life. What we don't always like is the patience that it takes to get us there. But like it or not, patience is part of God's process for growth. Patience plays a key role in some of the most powerful factors that shape our future:

1. *Making good decisions.*
2. *Cultivating a healthy soul.*
3. *Choosing to trust God.*

I like to call these "Future Factors." When consistently applied in our life, these three things will lead us forward and help us build a good future. Most importantly, they will help us build a life that honors God and brings us rewards of eternal significance.

Future Factor #1: Making good decisions.

Nothing is more powerful than being able to make good decisions. As I mentioned before, our decisions determine our direction and our direction determines our destiny. We are slowly but surely shaping our life and choosing our destination with the decisions we make on a daily basis. If we're not careful, impatience can cause us to make decisions in the moment that don't line up with where we want to go in life.

The reality is one impatient choice can put us on a big detour on the path of life. It may not prevent us from fulfilling our destiny and embracing all God has called us to be, but we may end up taking the long way to get there. It may also mean we have to live with the consequences of our choice.

If we want positive results in our life, we have to make positive, healthy choices. It's going to mean delaying gratification for the good of the big picture. Tough, but worth it.

Many years ago I heard a little phrase: "Live today with tomorrow in mind." This one little piece of wisdom has helped me significantly in the area of making good choices. Patience gives us the wisdom to slow down and ask ourselves the right questions before jumping right in and taking action. Here are some questions to help us make good decisions:

- *What does God's Word say?*
- *What is the wise thing to do?*
- *Do I have all the facts?*
- *What will the consequences of this decision be— for me and others?*
- *Should I get some wisdom from someone else?*
- *In light of my past experiences, my present situation, and my future vision, is this a wise choice?*

Impatience can distort our perspective. If you've ever shared a picture on social media, you might be familiar with how much a filter can change the look of it. It can take a great picture and make it look bad or take a bad picture and make it look good. Impatience does the same thing in our life. It puts a filter on the lens of our mind and can trick us into making a decision based on an altered perception of reality.

Take your time and make a good decision, especially on big ones. Don't get me wrong—not every decision is a major one! If you're at a restaurant trying to decide what to eat, just go ahead and pick something. But when it comes to big decisions in our life, like choosing who we are going to marry or if we will move to a new city, it's always worth being patient enough to make a wise decision.

Future Factor #2: Cultivating a healthy soul.

Third John 2 says, "Beloved, I pray that you may prosper in all things and be in health, just as your soul prospers" (NKJV). The health of our soul needs to be a priority in our life, because it's at the core of who we are and everything we do.

You'd probably agree that patience is one of the things a healthy soul produces in our life. And that's true, but patience is also part of God's prescription for how we can cultivate a healthy soul in the first place. Luke 21:19 says, "By your patience possess your souls" (NKJV).

Every single one of us will find ourselves in situations that weigh on our mind or upset our emotions or create tension in our will at some point. A patient person can withstand the pressures of life without letting them unravel their soul (their mind, emotions, and will). This patience allows them to think clearly, keep their attitude and emotions in check, and continue making good choices, even in tough times.

In 1886, William Bernard Ullathorne published a book composed of a series of lectures on patience called *Christian Patience, the Strength & Discipline of the Soul*. In one of his lectures, he wrote, "There can be no better proof of a healthy soul than habitual cheerfulness. Christian cheerfulness springs from charity and is protected by patience . . . patience that keeps the soul in peace, and protects the spring of cheerfulness from being troubled or diminished."[4]

To an impatient person, however, life quickly starts to feel out of control because their soul is out of control. The danger of letting our soul get away from us is that our mind, our emotions, and our will start getting ahead of us. Instead of being at peace, our soul goes into a frustrated state of overdrive. When this happens, the health of our soul starts to decline, and we can fall into a place of striving.

Striving is trying to accomplish God's will for our life in our own strength and on our own timeline. Here's the progression that takes place: an impatient soul becomes an unhealthy soul. An unhealthy soul leads to striving. Striving gets us out of sync with God's best.

A person with a healthy soul can trust God to build their life according to his plan, on his timeline. Psalm 127:1 says, "Unless the LORD builds the house, the builders labor in vain. Unless the LORD watches over the city, the guards stand watch in vain." What God builds, he sustains. The things we build in our own strength, we have to sustain.

This is an area where I have had to surrender to God many, many times over the years. Anyone who knows me will attest to the fact that I can be restless and impatient, always ready to take action. I have to be careful not to push forward in a season where God has said, "*Wait.*" Striving can never build the fullness of God's purpose in our life.

God has called us to keep moving forward in life, to keep taking our next steps, but we must keep a healthy soul so we don't misstep in the process. Patience enables us to keep waiting on God with a spirit of faith, even in the "wilderness" seasons we'd like to escape. As life coach Nancy Levin says, we have to "honor the space between no longer and not yet."[5] God doesn't waste a single season in our life. Even when we can't see it, he has a plan.

Has impatience crept into your soul and tipped you over into frustration and striving? Often it happens so gradually, we don't even realize it. Here are a few questions to ask yourself to help you know if you've crossed over into a place of striving:

- Is your mind at ease and at rest, or is it restless and unsettled?
- Are your emotions peaceful, or are you agitated, frustrated, and angry?
- Are your decisions Spirit-led, or are you trying to control and manipulate your circumstances?

A healthy soul can reach forward in faith yet rest happy, free, and content right now as it waits.

Worth the Wait

In 1972, Stanford University ran an experiment that placed individual children in a room with a marshmallow. They were told if they waited until the researcher conducting the test came back, they could have two marshmallows. Inevitably, some children gave in to their desire for immediate gratification, while others opted to delay gratification for the increased reward.

Years later, follow-up results revealed the children who were able to wait showed better outcomes later in life—better SAT scores, lower levels of substance abuse, greater competence, and improved social skills as well as a superior ability to handle stress, plan, and concentrate without becoming distracted.[6]

But researchers were still curious. What influenced the children's ability to wait patiently and hold out for the reward? To find the answer, the University of Rochester conducted another experiment. They created two groups of children and planned a series of interactions that would take place before the marshmallows were offered to the children. Prior to receiving marshmallows, the children in both groups were given the same craft to do. In one group, the researcher promised to go get better art supplies two different times. Each time, he or she came back without them. The second group received the same promise but the better art supplies were delivered as promised. The marshmallow experiment was then conducted.[7]

In the group where the researcher made good on his or her promise, the children were far more likely to wait the full length of time and receive the reward. In fact, they waited four times as long as the children whose researcher didn't make good on his or her promise.

The astonishing conclusion was this: *the greatest factor shaping the children's decision to wait was whether or not they trusted the person in charge.* More than hunger or any other factor impacting the results, their belief shaped their willingness to wait.

Isn't this so true in our life as well? When we believe that God is good, that he loves us, and that he has a good plan for our life, we have the strength and hope to keep waiting, even in the midst of challenging circumstances. But when we begin to question God's goodness and his love for us, our trust falters and we struggle to be patient. Because—if we're honest—we're just not sure it's going to be worth it. What we believe about God ultimately determines how we wait in the midst of situations we wish we could change.

The real question is: *Do you want your best now or God's best later?* When it comes down to it, a lot of our impatience is rooted in the belief that our plan for our life is better than God's. The key is choosing to believe God can be trusted with every part of our life.

Missionary Elisabeth Elliot lived this out so powerfully in her lifetime. Elisabeth and her husband Jim served as missionaries in Ecuador in the 1950s. They met in college and shared a passion for taking the gospel to the nations, especially people groups who had little exposure to the Bible.

After college, they separately pursued mission work in Ecuador, each convinced it was what God had called them to in that season. In 1953, after five years apart, they married in Ecuador and continued the work Jim had been doing among the Quichua Indians.

In the fall of 1955, one of Jim's friends who worked with missionary pilots came across a tiny Huaoroni Indian settlement in the jungle. The Huaoroni were also referred to as the *Auca* by neighboring tribes, a native word meaning "savage." Violence permeated every aspect of their culture. When a member of their tribe became old or ill, the others would topple their hammock and bury them alive. Male children were taught to kill at a young age, often for sport. *Time* magazine called them "the worst people on earth."[8] They were a tribe literally defined by a culture of death.

The Auca tribe were the pinnacle of unreached people in Ecuador—the kind of people Jim and his friends felt compelled to reach. Jim and four other missionaries decided they would take on the challenge of reaching out to the Auca and sharing the gospel. They prayed, planned, and strategized on how they could most effectively establish contact, researching other missionaries' techniques with similar tribes.

After much planning and preparing, they spent three months using airplanes to make low passes over the Auca's settlement, dropping gifts and supplies and calling out friendly phrases in their native language. In January 1956, they decided to make face-to-face contact with the tribe. But despite a friendly initial encounter, the second meeting turned violent and all radio contact was lost.

Five days later Elisabeth received the news her husband and the other men had been speared to death. She was devastated. They had waited five years to get married and now, after only two years of marriage, Jim was gone. After his death, Elisabeth decided to remain in Ecuador with their ten-month-old daughter, Valerie. She continued their work among the tribes, telling God if there was anything he would have her do for the Auca people, she would obey.

One day she unexpectedly met an Auca woman who had fled from her tribe. Through this woman, Elisabeth was able to reestablish connection with the Aucas. Two years after Jim was killed, she and three-year-old Valerie, along with the sister of one of the other missionaries, moved to live among the Auca people.

In the two years she spent there, Elisabeth saw many members of the once-violent tribe turn to Jesus, including some of the very same men who had murdered her husband. The pain of her greatest loss produced the seeds of her greatest victory: to bring the gospel to a people previously untouched by its message of hope and to inspire thousands of Christians around the world to devote their lives to radical mission work.[9]

Future Factor #3: Choosing to trust God.

One of the life messages Elisabeth Elliot carried was this: "The will of God is always different from what [we] expect; always bigger, and ultimately, infinitely more glorious than [our] wildest imaginings."[10]

When it comes down to it, patience is all about trusting God. This is where the "faith" part of "waiting on God with a spirit of faith" comes in. It's incredibly hard to trust God sometimes. Especially when life doesn't go as we thought it would.

We can start asking, *Has God forgotten me? Does he see the pain and frustration this is causing me? How on earth could this possibly be part of his plan?* Elisabeth wrestled through some of those exact moments of wondering and waiting. Later in life, on her radio program, she shared these wise words:

> When we are waiting on God . . . we do not have a time schedule in front of us. . . . Sometimes we think of our life as being on hold. I don't think waiting on God is a merely passive thing. And certainly it doesn't mean that our life is on hold. Every second of every minute of every hour of every day of every week of every month of every year we are meant to be living actively by faith. We're talking about trust. And every second is real.[11]

At so many points along the way, God's answer to my questions has been the same: *Trust me.* Some of the other words the Bible uses in place of *patience* are *forbearance*, *endurance*, *steadfastness*, and *perseverance*. When we look at all of these different words together, they convey the idea of being able to withstand resistance, a commitment to not give up in the middle of whatever we're facing, no matter how uncomfortable it gets. This is exactly what we have to do in the seasons when God is asking us to wait, to trust him.

This is tough. Really, *really* tough, sometimes. When we have to wait, it usually produces some sort of discomfort. So what do we do? We naturally look for ways to alleviate our discomfort. But what we don't realize is when we're out of our comfort zone, we're actually in position for God to do some of his most significant work in our life. James 1:2–4 says, "My brethren, count it all joy when you fall into various trials, knowing that the testing of your faith produces patience. But let patience have its perfect work, that you may be perfect and complete, lacking nothing" (NKJV).

The Living Bible says it this way: "When the way is rough, your patience has a chance to grow. So let it grow, and don't try to squirm out of your problems. For when your patience is finally in full bloom, then you will be ready for anything, strong in character, full and complete" (vv. 3–4).

This is what we have to remember: *while we are waiting on God, God is working in us.* He is building something deep down inside us that's of great and eternal value. There are some things that can only be worked into—or out of—our life through patience.

As Elisabeth Elliot weathered the different seasons of joy and grief, loss and triumph, she was able to come out on the other side with an incredible understanding of what it means to truly trust God. She wrote, "The deepest spiritual lessons are not learned by His letting us have our way in the end, but by His making us wait, bearing with us in love and patience until we are able to honestly pray what He taught His disciples to pray: 'Thy will be done.'"[12]

God's promises are always best on his timeline—not ours. We need to give it time and trust that God knows what he's doing. Patience prepares the promise for us and prepares us for the promise.

Maybe you find yourself in a place where you're struggling to trust God as you wait. Perhaps you're tired of a mundane season where it appears nothing is happening. Maybe you're in the midst of a painful situation, and you've been waiting so long that it feels like your hopes, dreams, and plans have gone up in smoke. Life has burned you, and now you're left holding a pile of smoldering ashes.

In the Bible, ashes represented mourning. But we find an incredibly reassuring promise in Isaiah 61:3: "To all who mourn in Israel, he will give a crown of beauty for ashes, a joyous blessing instead of mourning, festive praise instead of despair. In their righteousness, they will be like great oaks that the LORD has planted for his own glory" (NLT).

If you find yourself struggling to deal with some parts of your story that don't make sense or seem fair; if you're struggling to reconcile the realities of disappointments, failures, losses, or unanswered prayers with the goodness of God, find hope in these powerful words from Elisabeth Elliot: "Of one thing I am perfectly sure: God's story never ends with 'ashes.'"[13]

There may be some things we never fully understand on this side of eternity. What we can hold on to is the truth that even in the difficult times where our faith is tested, God can work in us and through us to produce something far more significant than we could ever imagine.

When life shatters our plans, we might look at them and see unusable, broken pieces with no apparent purpose left in them. But what we have to remember is there's a bigger picture we can't see—one that's coming together in every situation and season of life. Each piece has a place in the picture. We see the broken pieces, but God sees the big picture.

It's a mosaic where broken pieces are taken and transformed into a masterpiece.

There is always more happening than what we can see. Keep making good decisions, keep cultivating a healthy soul, and keep trusting God. Don't hate while you wait. While you are waiting, God is working.

Evaluate / Eliminate / Elevate

Evaluate: What areas of your life do you tend to get impatient about?

Eliminate: What specific doubts, questions, or frustrations do you need to release?

Elevate: Identify one area to focus on this week: making good decisions, cultivating a healthy soul, or trusting God. What is the biggest step you need to take in this area?

When our faith starts to waver, doubt and impatience can start to creep in. When this happens, we must always go back and hold on to the truth of God's Word.

Here are some of the truths we need to anchor ourselves in when we're in a place of waiting and trusting:

1. God is good (Ps. 100:5; 136:1).
2. He loves you—all the time, no matter what (Jer. 31:3; Rom. 8:38–39).
3. He will never leave you nor forsake you (Deut. 31:8; Isa. 43:2).
4. He has a good plan for your life. His plan is not to harm you, but to give you a future and a hope (Jer. 29:11).

Afterword

The Spirit of an Overcomer

> It is essential to understand that battles
> are won primarily in the hearts of men.
>
> *Bernard Law Montgomery*

Your heart is the battleground for your future. The reality is, as you pursue God's plan for your life, you might go through the fight of your life along the way. Remember Louie Zamperini? That was certainly the case for him. On the heels of his greatest achievement came the greatest fight he had encountered yet—the fight to survive.

After he had broken record after record across the nation and qualified for the 1936 Berlin Olympics, Louie's life took a sharp turn. World War II broke out and he, like many others of that generation, put his dreams on hold and enlisted in the service. In April 1943, while on a rescue mission with ten other men in the South Pacific, his plane suffered engine failure and crashed into the ocean. Only Louie and two others survived.

They managed to stay alive by floating in the open water on a raft, but the conditions were brutal. As the weeks passed, their faces blistered from the sun, their lips swelled until they reached their noses and chins. The men wasted away from starvation and dehydration, and one of them eventually died. As Louie and his friend lay in the raft, surrounded by sharks in the water beneath, they knew it was more crucial than ever to keep hope alive.

Finally, after surviving an unthinkable forty-seven days at sea and drifting a staggering two thousand miles, it appeared they were about to be rescued as a plane flew overhead. But their troubles were far from over. As one nightmare ended, a new one began. They were taken by the Japanese and put in prison, where they were starved, tortured, and abused mentally and physically. Their captors pushed them to their limits, and many times the circumstances felt unbearable.

There was one particularly violent incident with his captors that Louie knew was designed to break him. "But I couldn't give up hope," he said. "Not my style. I would do what I had to do to survive. From that moment until the end of the war, when we were freed, I would really come to understand the meaning of 'Don't give up, don't give in.'"[1]

The Will to Overcome

Most of us have never encountered the kind of challenges Louie Zamperini did. Most of us never will. Our challenges may be different, but God wants us to approach them with the same spirit he did: the spirit of an overcomer.

For some, it's the suffocating weight of a struggling business venture that keeps you up at night thinking, *What's going to happen if this goes under?* Others are wondering how to keep moving forward in life while grieving the loss of someone close or living with a chronic illness. Maybe your marriage—the one that used to be healthy and strong—is slowly coming apart at the seams. It's crumbling right before your eyes, and you have no idea what to do to stop it. In these times, we need an overcoming spirit to help sustain us.

But the need to overcome doesn't just happen when we face life-altering situations. We have to be able to overcome in the things that are bound to happen in everyday life too—when a deal falls through at work, when your car breaks down and you miss an important meeting, when you hit a rough patch in your parenting.

It doesn't matter how successful we are, how smart we are, or how much money we have. Everyone will encounter challenges and opposition at some point. The question is, *Will they overcome us, or will we overcome them?* We may face circumstances we don't have the power to change. Overcoming is not necessarily the change we bring to a situation but rather the spirit we maintain in the midst of it.

When we think about it, the Bible is a collection of the greatest stories ever told. It's the stuff that epic movies are made of: flawed heroes, impossible situations, and a costly act of redemption that changed the course of humanity's eternal future. Its impact rippled through generations and has been transforming lives ever since. Yes, if there ever was a story about overcoming, the Bible is it. But this story about overcoming isn't just one God intends us to read—it's one he intends us to *live*.

What we have to realize is that God created us to be overcomers (Rom. 8:37; 1 John 5:4). The story that we are part of is—and always has been—all about overcoming.

The Good Life

There are so many great verses about overcoming, but I want to focus on two in particular. Let's break down what they mean for us and then pull out the strategy they give us for overcoming and moving forward in life.

> Do not be overcome by evil, but overcome evil with good. (Rom. 12:21)

> And they overcame him by the blood of the Lamb and by the word of their testimony, and they did not love their lives to the death. (Rev. 12:11 NKJV)

The enemy will do everything in his power to take us out and keep us from fulfilling our purpose. But exactly how do we put "good" to work in our life so that we can overcome him? Matthew 12:35 tells us a good man "brings good things out of the good stored up in him."

The key to overcoming is to be consistently building good things into our life. We need to be preparing for victory long before we get to the battlefield. If we overcome in the moment, it is because we have put good things in along the way.

Here are three "good things" that prepare us for the battleground of life's challenges: a good spirit, a good support system, and a good strategy.

1. A good spirit.

A good spirit is a strong spirit. It can press forward in the face of resistance. Think about strength from a physical standpoint. Resistance doesn't diminish a muscle's strength; it builds it. A healthy spirit can not only endure resistance but actually gain strength from it.

As we press forward to overcome some of the hangups and issues that are holding us back, we'll face some resistance. We'll have to be able to endure a certain amount of strain on the way to achieving our goal. This applies spiritually, physically, mentally, and emotionally. If we have a strong spirit, it helps us have the inner fortitude we need to build strength in other areas of our life too—our mind, our emotions, even our physical bodies.

A good spirit is not only strong, it's also full of faith. When it comes to moving forward in life and in our relationship with God, nothing is more important than faith. Hebrews 11, the great "Hall of Faith" chapter, tells us without faith it is impossible to please God (v. 6) and that faith is "the title deed of the things we hope for" (v. 1, AMP-CE). Faith has the amazing ability to move the heart of God and compel him to act on our behalf (Mark 5:34).

Simply put, God's best for our life will always require faith. It is always beyond what we can understand or achieve on our own. Our own strength, our own wisdom, and our own abilities simply aren't enough. If we have some God-sized visions and dreams in our heart, we're going to need faith to see them come to fruition.

Finally, a good spirit is persevering and relentless. James 1:12 encourages us, "Blessed is the one who perseveres under trial because, having stood the test, that person will receive the crown of life that the Lord has promised to those who love him." If we truly believe God is who he says he is and can do what he says he will do, it will produce a persevering, relentless quality in our spirit. This isn't about personality—it's about spiritual and mental tenacity. It's about strength of character. It's about gritting our teeth and making the choice to keep going when we feel like giving up.

In his book *Your Road Map for Success*, leadership expert John Maxwell says, "Failure comes easily to everyone, but the price of success is perseverance."[2] If you are someone who doesn't quit, you will set yourself apart from the crowd.

In a tough season of life, you may feel like you're barely hanging on. Keep putting one foot in front of the other, day by day, minute by minute. Maybe you feel like you can't even do that. Even in those moments, you can still purpose to hold your ground and keep the progress you *have* made. Don't retreat and start taking steps backward. Sometimes the key to winning is to simply not quit. Whatever you do . . . just don't give up!

2. A good support system.

God designed us to function best in the context of healthy, life-giving relationships. Even Jesus spent his time on earth with a crew of people who were closely connected to his daily life. Proverbs 18:1 warns us that the person who keeps everyone at arm's length "cares only about himself. He argues against all good wisdom" (NLV).

If you don't have a good support system of people who can build you up, I strongly encourage you to make that a priority. Get planted in a life-giving church if you aren't already. Get involved! Serve, join a volunteer team, be a part of a small group. Be intentional about getting connected with godly people who are moving in the right direction.

Motivational speaker Jim Rohn famously said, "You are the average of the five people you spend the most time with."[3] The people with whom you spend time significantly shape who you become and where you go in life. What kind of people are you hanging out with? Who is speaking into your life and influencing your heart, your mind, and the direction of your life? Do you want your life to look like theirs?

As the saying goes, "Show me your friends and I'll show you your future." Poor relationship choices can destroy a life, but building healthy, life-giving friendships with godly people can help you go the distance and enjoy the journey in life.

3. A good strategy.

Remember the strategy Revelation 12:11 gives us for being able to overcome: "And they overcame him by the blood of the Lamb and by the word of their testimony, and they did not love their lives to the death" (NKJV). Let's break this down a little.

"The blood of the Lamb" tells us the power to overcome isn't found in our own strength, wisdom, or ability. It comes from the victory Christ won at the cross. In the Old Testament, a sacrifice was required to pay for the sins of the people. The blood was considered payment, and the people were forgiven and cleansed of their sins. Jesus's death on the cross was the final sacrifice, the ultimate payment for our sins as the perfect blood of a sinless man was shed. Because of that sacrifice, our sin can be wiped away. Sin and death no longer reign—they were defeated by Jesus's death and resurrection. The blood of Jesus is our lifeline to salvation, strength, wisdom, power, endurance, and hope we couldn't have any other way.

"The word of their testimony" is talking about the words we speak over our life. A confession is a declaration of something that is true. Romans 10:9–10 teaches us salvation comes through belief and confession. We believe in our heart Christ was raised from the dead and we also confess it with our mouth. Here's what I want to submit to you: if confession initiates salvation, then confession—the declaration of the truth we believe—is something that should continue throughout our Christian life to keep us walking in victory. The words we speak have powerful effects on our life, both positive and negative. Proverbs 18:21 cautions us, "What you say can preserve life or destroy it; so you must accept the consequences of your words" (GNT). In *The Message* this verse reads, "Words kill, words give life; they're either poison or fruit— you choose."

Get in a habit of speaking God's Word over your life. Speak it over your health, your mind, your future, your marriage, your kids, your job, everything! When Jesus was tempted, he responded to the enemy's attacks with, "It is written" (Matt. 4:4). The enemy is not afraid of our words—but he is afraid of *God's Word*. Learn God's Word. Pray it, speak it, and believe it—it changes things! (If you need help getting started, two great resources are Joyce Meyer's *The Secret Power of Speaking God's Word* and Germaine Copeland's *Prayers That Avail Much*.)

The third part of the strategy is something that creates a giant barrier for a lot of us: leaving our comfort zone. "They did not love their lives to the death" means our comfort zone cannot determine our course. You're probably thinking, *Hang on a second; this is talking about death and that's really intense.* Just track with me for a minute while we look at this. I'm not saying we have to die for Jesus to be a good Christian, but what we do see in this verse is that these believers hadn't placed any limits on what they were willing to do for Jesus. Nothing was beyond his reach; they were all in. Their comfort zone did not determine their commitment to Jesus.

Human nature naturally moves toward comfort and away from discomfort. But this is what I've learned: everything significant God has brought into my life was initiated when I made a willful decision to step into something uncomfortable.

When we moved to Africa, it was uncomfortable. Raising finances, leaving our families and friends, the actual process of moving over there, immersing ourselves in a new culture . . . every bit of it was completely out of our comfort zone. Then, when we moved to Memphis, that was tough too. Leslie and I both grew up in Baton Rouge, and with the exception of our time in Africa we'd lived there our entire lives. We were used to being around a lot of family and friends we'd known since we were children. It was an uncomfortable feeling to move back to the States to plant a church (something we'd never done) in a city where we didn't know a soul.

Twenty years later, our church is thriving, the dream we saw in our hearts has now become a reality, and I know beyond a shadow of a doubt I'm walking in God's purpose for my life. But there were a whole lot of uncertain, uncomfortable decisions along the way that led us to this point. Looking back now, I'm so glad Leslie and I didn't let the discomfort of stepping out in faith stop us from saying yes to the call that was on our life.

Great things were never born in comfort zones. We can't love our life so much we are unwilling to move forward when God calls. Don't let anything have such a tight grip on your life that it keeps you from responding to the Holy Spirit's leading. No earthly comfort is worth it. Living the purpose-filled life you were created for comes with a cost, but it's well worth the price. Choose to endure a little discomfort and press forward to take hold of a prize that will last forever.

Into the Arena

My hope and prayer is that, as you've read these chapters, you've been inspired to make some changes that will help you move forward into God's best. But I want to encourage you—don't be content just to be inspired. As Dale Carnegie once wrote, "Our problem isn't ignorance, it's inaction."[4] Inspiration is a wonderful thing, but inspiration without action doesn't produce results.

In 1910, Theodore Roosevelt delivered these passion-filled words in a speech entitled, "Citizenship in a Republic," more commonly known as, "The Man in the Arena":

> It is not the critic who counts; not the man who points out how the strong man stumbles, or where the doer of deeds could have done them better. The credit belongs to the man who is actually in the arena, whose face is marred by dust and sweat and blood; who strives valiantly; who errs, who comes short again and again, because there is no effort without error and shortcoming; but who does actually strive to do the deeds; who knows great enthusiasms, the great devotions; who spends himself in a worthy cause; who at the best knows in the end the triumph of high achievement, and who at the worst, if he fails, at least fails while daring greatly, so that his place shall never be with those cold and timid souls who neither know victory nor defeat.[5]

Roosevelt's words were more than a rousing speech; they were the story of his life. An acute case of asthma threatened his life as a baby and severely impaired his health as a child. As a young man, he suffered the deaths of his wife and mother in the same day, leaving him a single father to a baby girl just two days old. Time after time, Roosevelt had been flung into "the arena" of life. But instead of retreating to the sidelines, he met his challenges head-on with a relentless, almost ferocious determination to persevere in the face of difficulty. He knew that in the arena is where life's victories are won.

We cannot win and overcome if we choose to remain safely sheltered in the confines of our comfort zone—inspired but not in action. We may avoid discomfort but we will also deny ourselves victory. If we want to receive the prize, we must step out into the arena and be willing to fight life through.

Finish Strong

In his book *Devil at My Heels*, Louie Zamperini recalls what enabled him to triumph in the face of desperate, hopeless circumstances time and time again. He said, "I'd made it this far and refused to give up because all my life I had always finished the race."[6]

I think the apostle Paul probably would have liked fiery, persistent Louie. Paul talks about running frequently in his writing, and he likens our life as a Christian to a race. In 2 Timothy 4:7–8, as he is approaching the end of his life, Paul looks back on his "race"—the life he lived—and the reward it had prepared for him. He said, "I have fought the good fight, I have finished the race, I have kept the faith. Now there is in store for me the crown of righteousness." There's a sense of final satisfaction in these words, because Paul had given his all and was finishing strong.

He tells us plain and simple: we are in a fight. It's a good fight, but it's a fight nonetheless. I think Paul is reminding us if we want to finish strong, we've got to have a little bit of "fight" down on the inside of us too.

There will be seasons where pursuing God's best means engaging in the struggle to win the battle for our future. What we have to remember is the purpose is always greater than the struggle—and the struggle is worth it. An overcomer is someone who can keep their faith in the middle of the fight. When challenges come our way, we need to dig in our heels spiritually and say, "This is not going to take me out. I can, and I will, overcome this with God's help."

Win the battle in your heart first. We overcome when the fight inside us is greater than the fight around us. Stir up the passion to finish strong and press through the challenge and come out on the other side: better, stronger, and more like Christ.

Little by Little

Our family visited Peru recently, and while we were there we had an incredible opportunity to climb Machu Picchu. It was unbelievable to see the ancient ruins and be so high in the mountains that we could look out for miles. We had been staying in Lima, which meant it was going to be a little bit of work to get there. We had to take a short flight to a small town in the mountains called Cusco. Then we had to drive to the train station, take the train up into the mountain range, and once we got into the mountains, finally start our hike up Machu Picchu to see the sights.

It was spectacular. *But it was a process.*

The same is true when it comes to moving forward and overcoming the barriers to God's best in our life. Don't be discouraged if it takes you awhile to make progress. Success isn't something that happens in a day; it's something that happens daily. Most likely, there will be some mountains you'll have to climb along the way.

A lot of times we pray and pray and pray for God to move the mountain so we can keep moving forward. And sometimes God does a miracle and moves the mountains in our life suddenly. But sometimes he doesn't. Sometimes he wants to use the mountain to grow our life, so instead of intimidating us and blocking our progress, it becomes a stepping stone to something greater. Ask and believe for the miracle, but don't set up camp if he tells you to start climbing!

Sure, it would be a whole lot easier if he would just instantly clear out all the obstacles holding us back. But honestly, God usually leads us forward into his best in a different way. When the Israelites finally arrived at the Promised Land after their journey through the wilderness, they didn't get to just walk into it and start their new life. There were obstacles to be overcome and enemies to be defeated. Exodus 23:30 tells us God drove out their enemies "little by little." The Promised Land was already theirs, but taking possession was a process. This process allowed them to build the strength they needed in order to thrive in their new home.

God's plan for our life unfolds little by little, step by step. I'm so thankful God is more patient with me than I am with him. When we're trying to move forward, it's easy to get ahead of ourselves or get discouraged when things don't change overnight. Just keep taking the step in front of you today . . . and tomorrow . . . and the next day . . . and the day after that. There's a Peruvian proverb that says, "Little by little, one walks far."[7] One day you'll look up and realize just how far God has brought you.

Yes, there will be challenges. You will face resistance along the way. But with the spirit of an overcomer, you can rise above them. As Dr. Martin Luther King Jr. said in his powerful speech entitled "Keep Moving from This Mountain," "If you can't fly, run, if you can't run, walk, if you can't walk, crawl, but by all means keep moving."[8]

Appendix

Budget Guide

Here are some basic budget categories and average percentages to help serve as a guideline as you establish a budget. The percentages listed represent the *total amount* of your spendable income that goes toward that category.

To calculate your spendable income, add up your total income each month and deduct your monthly tithe and offerings, taxes, and money to establish a $1,000 emergency fund if you do not have one. Once you have established your $1,000 emergency fund, it no longer needs to be taken out of your total income at the beginning of each month, but it is wise to make sure that you continue to save.

Total income: .... $ _____

—Tithe (10%): .... $ _____

—Taxes: .... $ _____

—Emergency Fund: .... $ _____

Spendable Income: .... $ _____

Take your spendable income and apply the following percentages to come up with a basic guideline for your monthly budget.

(Note: It's important to account for the different costs that may fall under each category. For example, your transportation category needs to account for more than just your car payment; you have to take into consideration your car insurance, gas, repairs, and yearly fees for taxes and registration.)

Housing (32%) . . . . $ _____

Food/Grocery (15%) . . . . $ _____

Transportation (15%) . . . . $ _____

Life Insurance (2%) . . . . $ _____

Clothing (5%) . . . . $ _____

Debts (5%) . . . . $ _____

Savings (5%) . . . . $ _____

Medical (7%) . . . . $ _____

Gifts (2%) . . . . $ _____

Entertainment/Recreation (7%) . . . $ _____

Miscellaneous (5%) . . . . $ _____

These percentages are recommendations to serve as a guideline and help you get started. Each person or family is different, and you can adjust the percentages as needed to fit your particular needs. But remember, if you increase one category's percentage, you've got to compensate by lowering another. *The bottom line in successful budgeting is that your total percentages must always add up to 100 percent.*

For more in-depth teaching on finances, I encourage you to check out a short book I wrote called *Worry Free Finances.*

Additional Resources

Online Resources

Crown Financial Ministries, www.crown.org
Dave Ramsey, www.daveramsey.com
Master Your Money, www.masteryourmoney.com

Books

Dave Ramsey, *Financial Peace*
Ron Blue, *Master Your Money*

Acknowledgments

I want to say thanks and acknowledge two amazing people I have the privilege of working alongside: Aimée Farmer and Katie Welch have spent countless hours organizing, writing, and editing this project. They are a key part of our team here at The Life Church, and in addition to their regular responsibilities they went above and beyond to make this book a reality.

Notes

Introduction

1. Gordon MacDonald, *Ordering Your Private World* (Nashville: Thomas Nelson, 2007), Kindle ed., 167.

2. Kathi Lipp, *Clutter Free* (Eugene, OR: Harvest House, 2015), 71.

Chapter 1 The Blame Game

1. Steve Carell and Helena De Bertodano, "Steve Carell Interview for *Despicable Me 2*," *The Telegraph*, June 27, 2013, http://www.telegraph.co.uk/culture/film/starsandstories/10129434/Steve-Carell-interview-for-Despicable-Me-2-Were-you-expecting-me-to-be-funny.html.

2. Charles R. Swindoll, "The Value of a Positive Attitude," *Insight For Today*, November 19, 2015, http://www.insight.org/resources/daily-devotional/individual/the-value-of-a-positive-attitude.

3. As quoted in John C. Maxwell, *Jump Start Your Growth: A 90-Day Improvement Plan* (New York: Center Street, 2015), Kindle ed., 587–88.

4. Brian Tracy, *No Excuses! The Power of Self-Discipline* (New York: Vanguard Press, 2010), 58.

5. Jim Collins, "Level 5 Leadership: The Triumph of Humility and Fierce Resolve," *Harvard Business Review*, July/August 2005, https://hbr.org/2005/07/level-5-leadership-the-triumph-of-humility-and-fierce-resolve/ar/1.

6. Dirk G. J. Panhuis, *Latin Grammar* (Ann Arbor: University of Michigan Press, 2006), 12.

7. Maya Angelou, *Letter to My Daughter* (New York: Random House, 2008), 3.

8. Stephen R. Covey, *The 7 Habits of Highly Effective People: Restoring the Character Ethic* (New York: Free Press, 2004), 71.

Chapter 2 Steady On

1. Caroline Leaf, *Who Switched Off My Brain? Controlling Toxic Thoughts and Emotions* (Southlake, TX: Inprov, 2009), 89.

2. Neil T. Anderson, *Victory Over the Darkness: Realizing the Power of Your Identity in Christ* (Ventura, CA: Regal Books, 1990), 156.

3. As quoted in Don Colbert, *Deadly Emotions: Understand the Mind-Body-Spirit Connection That Can Heal or Destroy You* (Nashville: Thomas Nelson, 2003), Kindle ed., 9.

4. Ibid.

5. Ibid.

6. Bradford A. Mullen, "Sanctification," *Evangelical Dictionary of Biblical Theology*, ed. Walter A. Elwell (Grand Rapids: Baker Books, 1996), accessed January 29, 2016, http://www.biblestudytools.com/dictionaries/bakers-evangelical-dictionary/sanctification.html.

7. Dallas Willard, *Renovation of the Heart: Putting On the Character of Christ* (Colorado Springs, CO: NavPress, 2002), Kindle ed., 2416.

8. Charles F. Stanley, *Success God's Way: Achieving True Contentment and Purpose* (Nashville: Thomas Nelson, 2000), 155.

9. Elisabeth Kübler-Ross and David Kessler, *Life Lessons: Two Experts on Death and Dying Teach Us about the Mysteries of Life and Living* (New York: Scribner, 2000), 118–19.

10. Ibid.

Chapter 3 Winning over Worry

1. Billy Graham, Franklin Graham, and Donna Lee Toney, *Billy Graham in Quotes* (Nashville: Thomas Nelson, 2011), 22.

2. Richard Hillyer, *Divided between Carelessness and Care: A Cultural History* (New York: Palgrave Macmillan, 2013), 8.

3. L. D. Kubzansky et al., "Is Worrying Bad for Your Heart?: A Prospective Study of Worry and Coronary Heart Disease in the Normative Aging Study," *Circulation* vol. 95, no. 4 (February 18, 1997): 818–24, http://circ.ahajournals.org/content/95/4/818.full.

4. Don Colbert, *Deadly Emotions: Understand the Mind-Body-Spirit Connection That Can Heal or Destroy You* (Nashville: Thomas Nelson, 2003), Kindle ed., 103.

5. Ibid., 6.

6. Steve Sisgold, "De-Stress on Demand," *Psychology Today*, March 13, 2014, https://www.psychologytoday.com/blog/life-in-body/201403/de-stress-demand.

7. Dale Carnegie, *How to Stop Worrying and Start Living* (New York: Simon and Schuster, 2010), Kindle ed., 170–72.

8. Robert L. Leahy, *The Worry Cure: Seven Steps to Stop Worry from Stopping You* (New York: Harmony Books, 2005), 18.

9. Corrie ten Boom, *Clippings from My Notebook: Writings and Sayings Collected* (Nashville: Thomas Nelson, 1982), 32.

Chapter 4 So Long, Stinkin' Thinkin'

1. John Locke, *An Essay Concerning Human Understanding*, vol. 1, edited by Alexander C. Fraser (Oxford: Clarendon Press, 1894), 66.

2. Leaf, *Who Switched Off My Brain?*, 120.

3. Ibid., 40.

4. Ibid., 120.

5. James Allen, *Above Life's Turmoil* (New York: Cosimo Classics, 2007), 36.

6. Martin Luther and James C. Galvin, *Faith Alone: A Daily Devotional* (Grand Rapids: Zondervan, 2005), 8.

7. Leaf, *Who Switched Off My Brain?*, 30.

8. Joyce Meyer, "You Can Win the Battle in Your Mind," *Battlefield of the Mind—Teaching*, March/April 2011, http://www.joycemeyer.org/EverydayAns wers/teachings/teachingbotm.aspx?article=battlefield.

9. As quoted in Peter Economy, "21 Positive Quotes That Will Powerfully Influence Your Life and Work," *Inc.com*, September 10, 2015, http://www.inc.com/peter-eco nomy/21-positive-quotes-that-will-powerfully-influence-your-life-and-work.html.

10. Leaf, *Who Switched Off My Brain?*, 47.

11. As quoted in Jonathan Parnell, "100 Quotes from You on Sanctification," *Desiring God*, June 29, 2012, http://www.desiringgod.org/articles/100-quotes-from -you-on-sanctification.

12. As quoted in Jay W. West, *Willing to Yield* (Houston: Spirit Truth, 2013), Kindle ed., 2125–26.

13. As quoted in Noah Brooks, *Lincoln Observed: Civil War Dispatches of Noah Brooks*, ed. Michael Burlingame (Baltimore: Johns Hopkins University Press, 1998).

14. Andrew B. Newberg and Mark Robert Waldman, *How God Changes Your Brain: Breakthrough Findings from a Leading Neuroscientist* (New York: Ballantine Books, 2009), 26–27.

15. Caroline Leaf, "How Prayer Affects the Brain," *Dr. Leaf*, June 1, 2015, http://drleaf.com/blog/how-prayer-affects-the-brain/.

16. Anthony Martino, "Testimony," email message to the author, October 9, 2014, reprinted by permission.

Chapter 5 Time to Press Reset

1. As quoted in Tom Corr, *2,320 Funniest Quotes: The Most Hilarious Quips and One-liners from Allgreatquotes.com* (Berkeley, CA: Ulysses, 2011), 229.

2. Beth Han et al, "Receipt of Services for Behavioral Health Problems: Results from the 2014 National Survey on Drug Use and Health," *SAMHSA*, accessed January 30, 2016, http://www.samhsa.gov/data/sites/default/files/NSDUH-DR -FRR3-2014/NSDUH-DR-FRR3-2014/NSDUH-DR-FRR3-2014.htm.

3. As quoted in Philip Schaff, ed. *Nicene and Post-Nicene Fathers: First Series*, vol. 7 (Edinburgh: T&T Clark, 1888), 198.

4. As quoted in Kelly Nickell, ed. *Pocket Patriot: Quotes from American Heroes* (Cincinnati, OH: Writer's Digest Books, 2005), 196.

5. As quoted in Lewis Howes, "10 Lessons for Entrepreneurs from Coach John Wooden," *Forbes*, October 19, 2012, http://www.forbes.com/sites/lewishowes/2012 /10/19/10-lessons-for-entrepreneurs-from-coach-john-wooden/.

Chapter 6 Restricted Access

1. As quoted in Tara Koellhoffer, *Dealing with Frustration and Anger* (New York: Chelsea House, 2009), 43.

2. W. Robertson Nicoll, ed., *The Expositor's Greek Testament*, vols. 1–4 (New York: George H. Doran Company, 1911).

3. John C. Barefoot, Grant W. Dahlstrom, and Redford B. Williams, "Hostility, CHD Incidence, and Total Mortality: A 25-Year Follow-Up Study of 255 Physicians," *Psychosomatic Medicine* 45, no. 1 (March 1983): 59–63.

4. Colbert, *Deadly Emotions*, 118.

5. Maria Konnikova, "The Lost Art of the Unsent Angry Letter," *New York Times*, March 22, 2014, http://www.nytimes.com/2014/03/23/opinion/sunday/the-lost-art-of-the-unsent-angry-letter.html?_r=0.

6. Colbert, *Deadly Emotions*, 53–56.

7. Edward Bulwer-Lytton, *Caxtoniana: A Series of Essays on Life, Literature and Manners* (New York: Harper & Brothers, 1868), 210.

Chapter 7 Unlock the Door (and Throw Away the Key)

1. "Timeline," *Nelson Mandela Foundation*, accessed January 30, 2016, https://www.nelsonmandela.org/content/page/timeline.

2. As quoted in Nadia Bilchik, "A White South African's Memories of Mandela," *CNN*, June 18, 2013, http://www.cnn.com/2013/06/14/opinion/bilchik-nelson-mandela/.

3. Strong's Greek Concordance, "4625. (skandalon)," *Bible Hub*, accessed January 30, 2016, http://biblehub.com/greek/4625.htm.

4. *Invictus*, directed by Clint Eastwood (Burbank, CA: Warner Brothers Studios, 2009), DVD.

5. Colbert, *Deadly Emotions*, 122.

6. "Forgive: Definition of Forgive," Oxford Dictionary (US English), accessed January 30, 2016, http://www.oxforddictionaries.com/us/definition/american_english/forgive.

7. Corrie ten Boom, "I'm Still Learning to Forgive," *Guideposts*, November 1972.

8. Martin Luther King Jr., Susan Carson, and Clayborne Carson, *The Papers of Martin Luther King, Jr.* 2nd ed., vol. 4 (Los Angeles: University of California Press, 2000), 321.

9. Martin Luther King Jr., "Loving Your Enemies," speech, Dexter Avenue Baptist Church, Montgomery, Alabama, December 25, 1957, http://www.thekingcenter.org/blog/mlk-quote-week-sticking-love.

Chapter 8 Believe Big, Hustle Hard

1. Louis Zamperini and David Rensin, *Don't Give Up, Don't Give In: Lessons from an Extraordinary Life*, reprint ed. (Dey Street Books, 2014), 18.

2. Ibid., 19.

3. Ibid., 26.

4. "Rocky," *New York Times*, November 1, 1976, https://www.nytimes.com/packages/html/movies/bestpictures/rocky-ar.html.

5. "Diligence—Dictionary Definition," Vocabulary.com, accessed January 30, 2016, https://www.vocabulary.com/dictionary/diligence.

6. "Diligence," *Webster's Revised Unabridged Dictionary* (Springfield, MA: C & G Merriam Co., 1913).

7. "Negate—Dictionary Definition," *Merriam-Webster*, accessed January 30, 2016, http://www.merriam-webster.com/dictionary/negate.

8. "Details Matter," *NBC News*, February 24, 2014, http://www.nbcnews.com/tech/tech-news/details-matter-apples-tim-cook-steve-jobs-59th-birthday-n37221.

9. Lee Cockerell, *Time Management Magic: How to Get More Done Every Day, Move from Surviving to Thriving* (Tulsa, OK: Emerge, 2014), Kindle ed., 169–70.

10. Robert Frost, *North of Boston* (New York: H. Holt and Co., 1915), chapter 9, line 56.

11. Zamperini and Rensin, *Don't Give Up, Don't Give In*, 30–33.

12. Jim Collins, "Good to Great," *Jim Collins*, October 2001, http://www.jimcollins.com/article_topics/articles/good-to-great.html.

Chapter 9 The Seven Pillars of Financial Wisdom

1. Melissa Chan, "Here's How Winning the Lottery Makes You Miserable," *Time*, January 12, 2016, http://time.com/4176128/powerball-jackpot-lottery-winners/.

2. Kathryn Buschman Vasel, "Why We Overspend," *Fox Business*, June 12, 2012, http://www.foxbusiness.com/features/2012/06/01/why-overspend.html.

3. Ibid.

4. Martha C. White, "Today's Young Adults Will Never Pay Off Their Credit Card Debts," *Time*, January 17, 2013, http://business.time.com/2013/01/17/todays-young-adults-will-never-pay-off-their-credit-card-debts/.

5. Elyssa Kirkham, "1 in 4 Americans' No. 1 Daily Thought Is Money, Survey Finds," *MSN Money*, September 9, 2015, http://www.msn.com/en-us/money/personalfinance/1-in-4-americans'-no-1-daily-thought-is-money-survey-finds/ar-AAe6r30?li=BBgzzfc.

6. Norman B. Anderson, PhD, and Cynthia D. Belar, PhD, *Stress in America: Paying With Our Health*, report, American Psychological Association, 2014.

7. Ibid.

8. Dave Ramsey, "The Bible and Money—Church Curriculum," accessed January 31, 2016, http://www.daveramsey.com/church/scriptures/ictid/church1/.

9. Robert T. Kiyosaki and Sharon L. Lechter, *Rich Dad, Poor Dad: What the Rich Teach Their Kids about Money—That the Poor and Middle Class Do Not!* (New York: Warner Business Books, 2000), 56.

10. "Dictionary Definition: Tithe," *Merriam-Webster*, accessed January 31, 2016, http://www.merriam-webster.com/dictionary/tithe.

11. "The American Heritage Dictionary Entry: Plowed," *American Heritage Dictionary*, accessed January 31, 2016, https://ahdictionary.com/word/search.html?q=plowed.

12. Theodore Roosevelt, "Address to the New York State Agricultural Association, Syracuse, NY," September 7, 1903, *The American Presidency Project*, March 6, 2016, http://www.presidency.ucsb.edu/ws/?pid=24504.

13. Jonathan Swift and Walter Scott, *The Works of Jonathan Swift, Containing Additional Letters, Tracts, and Poems Not Hitherto Published; with Notes and a Life of the Author* (Edinburgh: A. Constable, 1814), 449.

14. Thomas J. Stanley and William D. Danko, *The Millionaire Next Door: The Surprising Secrets of America's Wealthy* (Atlanta, GA: Longstreet Press, 1996), 228, emphasis added.

15. As quoted in National Archives, "Instructions to Company Captains, 29 July 1757," *Founders Online*, last updated March 28, 2016, http://founders.archives.gov/documents/Washington/02-04-02-0223.

16. Dave Ramsey, "6 Quotes That Will Make You Smarter Today," accessed January 20, 2016, https://www.daveramsey.com/blog/6-quotes-smarter-today.

17. Dave Ramsey, "When You Base Your Life on Principle, 99% of Your Decisions Are Already Made," Twitter post, March 18, 2013, https://twitter.com/ramseyshow/status/313679396991016960.

Chapter 10 Don't Hate While You Wait

1. As quoted in George Fuller, *I Golf, Therefore I Am—Nuts!* (Champaign, IL: Human Kinetics, 2009), 8.

2. Dave Nussbaum, "Why Good Things Come to Those Who . . . Wait," *Capital Ideas*, July 1, 2013, http://www.chicagobooth.edu/capideas/magazine/summer-2013/good-things-come.

3. "Patience," *Virtue First Foundation*, accessed January 31, 2016, http://virtuefirst.org/virtues/patience/.

4. William Bernard Ullathorne, *Christian Patience, the Strength & Discipline of the Soul: A Course of Lectures* (London: Burns & Oates, 1886), 232.

5. Nancy Levin, "Is It Time for a Graceful Exit?" June 24, 2015, http://www.nancylevin.com/is-it-time-for-a-graceful-exit/.

6. American Psychological Association, "What You Need to Know about Willpower: The Psychological Science of Self-Control," accessed January 21, 2016, http://www.apa.org/helpcenter/willpower.aspx.

7. Celeste Kidd, Holly Palmeri, and Richard N. Aslin, "Rational Snacking: Young Children's Decision-Making on the Marshmallow Task Is Moderated by Beliefs about Environmental Reliability," *Cognition* 126, no. 1 (January 2013): 109–14.

8. "Ecuador: Mission to the Aucas," *Time*, January 23, 1956, http://time.com/vault/issue/1956-01-23/page/32/.

9. "Jim Elliot Biography," Wheaton College, accessed January 30, 2016, http://www.wheaton.edu/isae/hall-of-biography/jim-elliot.

10. Elisabeth Elliot, "The Supremacy of Christ," *The Elisabeth Elliot Newsletter*, March/April 1993, http://www.elisabethelliot.org/newsletters/march-april-93.pdf.

11. Elisabeth Elliot, "Waiting on God," *Gateway to Joy Radio Program* (Good News Broadcasting Association, Inc.), February 19, 1998.

12. Elisabeth Elliot, *Passion and Purity* (Grand Rapids: Revell, 2002), 89.

13. Elisabeth Elliot, *These Strange Ashes* (New York: Harper & Row, 1975), 145.

Afterword

1. Zamperini and Rensin, *Don't Give Up, Don't Give In*, 70.

2. John C. Maxwell, *Your Road Map for Success* (Nashville: Thomas Nelson, 2002), 137.

3. "Jim Rohn—The Law of Average," YouTube video, 6:49, posted by Marco Christen on March 8 2016, https://www.youtube.com/watch?v=DMmz-_MLudQ.

4. Dale Carnegie, *How to Stop Worrying and Start Living* (New York: Simon and Schuster, 2010), Kindle ed., preface.

5. Theodore Roosevelt, "Citizenship in a Republic," speech delivered at the Sorbonne, Paris, April 23, 1910, accessed January 22, 2016, http://www.theodo rerooseveltcenter.org/Learn-About-TR/TR-Encyclopedia/Culture-and-Society /Man-in-the-Arena.aspx.

6. Louis Zamperini and David Rensin, *Devil at My Heels* (New York: Harper-Collins, 2009), Kindle ed., 1840–41.

7. Deborah L. Kopka, Nancy Klepper, and Ann Edmonds, *Central & South America* (Dayton, OH: Lorenz Educational Press, 2011), 137.

8. Martin Luther King Jr., "Keep Moving from This Mountain," address at Spelman College, Atlanta, Georgia, April 10, 1960, accessed January 31, 2016, https://swap.stanford.edu/20141218225553/http://mlk-kpp01.stanford.edu/pri marydocuments/Vol5/10Apr1960_KeepMovingfromThisMountain,Addressat SpelmanCollege.pdf.

John Siebeling has a passion to develop leaders and help people move forward in life. He is the author of *Momentum* and *Worry Free Finances*. John's teaching brings insight and encouragement to thousands through his regional television program. John and his wife, Leslie, are the founding and lead pastors of The Life Church, located in the metro Memphis, Tennessee, area. The Life Church is a diverse, multi-campus church that has been named one of the fastest growing churches in America. John and Leslie love living life to the full with their two children, Anna and Mark.

ALSO AVAILABLE FROM
JOHN SIEBELING

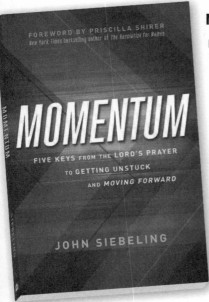

MOMENTUM

Many of us spend our lives struggling to move past the things that hold us back, but God has given us the keys to move forward in life. Discover five principles found in the Lord's Prayer that will help you move forward.

WORRY FREE FINANCES

Learn principles that allow you to lay a strong financial foundation, manage your resources wisely, and receive the blessings that come with living a generous, openhanded life.

LIKE THIS
BOOK?
Consider sharing it with others!

- Share or mention the book on your social media platforms. Use the hashtag **#MoveForwardBook**.

- Write a book review on your blog or on a retailer site.

- Pick up a copy for friends, family, or strangers— anyone who you think would enjoy and be challenged by its message!

- Share this message on Twitter or Facebook:
  I loved #MoveForwardBook by @JohnSiebeling @ReadBakerBooks

- Recommend this book for your church, workplace, book club, or class.

- Follow Baker Books on social media and tell us what you like.

 Facebook.com/ReadBakerBooks

 @ReadBakerBooks